GUIDE TO
California Wines

GUIDE TO

California Wines

BY JOHN MELVILLE

REVISED BY JEFFERSON MORGAN

E. P. DUTTON & CO., INC.

New York

To the memory

of

Joseph Henry Jackson

who first made this book possible

and

To the memory

of

James Pomeroy Howe

foreign correspondent, bon vivant,
winemaker, pigeon raiser, turkey smoker
and God knows what else, who encouraged
its revision

ACKNOWLEDGMENTS
TO THE FOURTH EDITION

To: *James F. Guymon,* Professor of Enology, and *Harold Olmo,* Professor of Viticulture at the University of California, Davis, for carefully rechecking Part I of the *Guide* and suggesting changes and additions;

California's *winemakers, winery owners* and others in and around the industry who responded to our many questions;

my wife, *Jinx,* who, at the moment I'm writing this, is busily numbering the pages of the manuscript at the same time she's trying to cook dinner.

JEFFERSON MORGAN

ACKNOWLEDGMENTS
TO THE SECOND EDITION

To: *Dr. A. Dinsmoor Webb,* Associate Professor of Enology, College of Agriculture, University of California, for his kindness in checking Part I of the *Guide* from the enological and viticultural points of view;

the *Wine Advisory Board* for permission to use the California wine map;

the *Wine Institute* for the list of Wineries that are open to the public (Chapter XVII) and other material;

Roy W. Taylor, Public Relations Director, Wine Institute, for his unfailing cooperation;

the *Owners* and/or *Managers* of the various wineries mentioned in the *Guide,* for their cooperation in checking the text concerning them and for supplying much useful information;

my wife, *Willy,* for her sage advice and assistance in getting the work done.

JOHN MELVILLE

PREFACE TO THE FOURTH EDITION

AT THE TIME of his death, John Melville was planning another revision of this *Guide*. His passing and the popularity of the second edition postponed it. However, as wineries went out of existence and others were founded, and as personalities and products changed, it became obvious a completely updated version was overdue. The job was undertaken in 1968 on assignment from the publisher, and again in 1971.

Baron John Melville-Van-Carnbee, who simplified his name for the purposes of authorship, was something of a crusader who wanted every man and woman in America to know the delights of California wines. It was an ambitious mission, but one which he undertook with gusto.

Born at The Hague, the son of a Dutch diplomat, John Melville gained his discerning appreciation of fine wines in his father's cellar. He became a Doctor of International Law, lecturer and author of a work on social economics. During World War II he fought with the infantry and air forces of the Free Netherlands Army, ending up as a lieutenant colonel, and was posted to Washington by his government between 1945 and 1950.

It was after that he moved to Carmel and began writing this book, a task he believed would be completed in a year. It actually took four to compile the basic information, although, in his own words, "a pleasanter, more convivial form of literary endeavor would be hard to imagine."

Every effort has been made to preserve the original author's Old World literary style, not an entirely simple chore in view of his diverse linguistic background. We hope we have been successful.

In the second edition John Melville warned that in spite of the help and assistance of those persons and organizations mentioned in the acknowledgments, errors of fact or judgment will undoubtedly have crept into the text. We repeat his invitation for correspondence to correct them.

San Francisco, California

PREFACE TO THE SECOND EDITION

THIS NEW EDITION of the *Guide to California Wines* makes its appearance due to popular demand. Designed as a practical reference volume for both the trade and the public, its aim is to present the wines of California in a comprehensive, accurate and interesting manner. So little information is available on this fascinating subject in book form. To fill that need is the purpose of this work. It has been completely rewritten and brought up to date. Much new material has been added.

California wines have come of age. Only the uninformed will deny that they have their own and diversified charm. The best of them, actually, match in quality, character and flavor all but the very finest estate bottled wines of France and Germany and are much more reasonable in price. Any host can be proud of serving them, even at the most formal occasion. A wine does not have to be imported to be really good. The savoring of a fine Cabernet Sauvignon or Pinot Noir will readily prove the fact. If the inevitable snob is not to be convinced, remove the label first. Better still, remove the snob!

California produces wines as different as the grapes from which they are produced and, as climate and soil, vary according to region. PART I of this volume describes the various kinds of wines produced, grouped according to their overall type. PART II tells about the more notable wineries producing directly for the public while listing their best known brands. PART III discusses, chartwise, the serving of wine and glasses. Here too will be found a listing of California wines especially recommended because of their outstanding character and a list of wineries that are open to the public. *Bon voyage!*

The author hopes that the reader will derive as much satisfaction from consulting the *Guide* as he had pleasure in composing it. He trusts also that the day is not far off when the United States of America, one of the great wine producing countries of the world, will adopt the serving of a glass or two of wine with the evening meal as a natural and national custom. So enjoyable and healthful a habit will do much to relax the personal tensions of the day and to promote feelings of well being and goodwill.

Casa Carnbee
Carmel-by-the-Sea, California

CONTENTS

Part Three

DRAWINGS

CHARTS

CALIFORNIA VINES AND WINES

CALIFORNIA WINES are produced from vines imported from Europe or from neighboring regions, and belonging to the Old World *Vitis vinifera* species of grapes.

The art of wine making was brought to California by the Spaniards. From Mexico wine growing spread northward to Baja California and finally to what was then known as Alta California. According to tradition, Padre Junipero Serra, of Mission fame, brought the first wines from Baja California and planted them at Mission San Diego in or about 1769. The Franciscan Fathers planted vines near the various Missions they established along their Camino Real stretching northward to Sonoma. The oldest California winery is to be found at Mission San Gabriel, where the famed Trinity Vine, planted around 1775, flourished for over a century and a half. It was from San Gabriel that settlers set forth one day to establish the Pueblo which was to become the city of Los Angeles.

The Mission Fathers planted what became known as the Mission grape, popular for long and still used today, mainly in the production of dessert wines.

The first layman wine grower of record was Governor Pedro Fages, who planted a vineyard along with his orchards in 1783, not far from his residence in Monterey, Alta California. Dona Marcelina

Felix Dominguez, the first known woman wine grower of California, planted, in the early eighteen hundreds, at Montecito near Santa Barbara, a fabulous vine which was to bear in good years some four tons of grapes. Known as *La Vieja de la Parra Grande,* or "The Old Lady of the Grapevine," she was said to be 105 years old when she died in 1865.

For a time Los Angeles led the rest of California in wine growing. There Joseph Chapman, an early immigrant, is conceded to have been the first viticulturist. He is far overshadowed in fame by Jean Louis Vignes, a native of the Bordeaux region in France and the possessor of a most appropriate name. By 1843 his celebrated Aliso Vineyard, in the heart of what is now downtown Los Angeles and named after a large sycamore which dominated the entrance to his property, covered over a hundred acres. Don Louis del Aliso, as he became known, was the first to import choice vines from Europe and to realize the great future of California wines, produced from these varieties. Many of his relatives followed him from France, including Pierre Sanssevain, who became a well-known grower in his own right.

In the northern region the first great wine growing pioneer was General Mariano Guadalupe Vallejo. Born in Monterey of Castilian descent he rose to prominence at an early age, becoming closely identified with the Mexican and early American history of California and especially with that of Sonoma, where he resided for many years. He was a great gentleman, farmer, soldier and philosopher. He accepted the "manifest destiny" whereby Alta California, in its own interest and by the force of circumstances, was to become part of the United States. In June 1846 a company of Americans ran up the Bear Flag in the plaza of Sonoma and soon afterward the American Army raised the flag of the United States. Vallejo, in spite of a brief incarceration by the overly patriotic Bears, accepted the new regime. He continued to devote himself to his agricultural pursuits and to aid immigrant Yankees to settle in the newly opened region. He was the first non-missionary wine grower in the Sonoma Valley and dominated the viticultural scene there for many years, until the advent of Haraszthy.

Colonel Agoston Haraszthy is often referred to as "the father of California's modern wine industry." It is greatly owing to his genius that a sound and lasting basis was created for the state's viticulture. It is a pleasing thought that the wine growing estate near Sonoma, which Haraszthy called Buena Vista and made famous, is in operation today. It is there that some of the story of this colorful California wine growing pioneer will be found.

California wineries have a long and proud tradition. Many of the better-known enterprises flourishing today were founded in the nineteenth century, some still being run by members of the founding family. Their listing by county and in approximate chronological order, according to the owners' claims, presents an intriguing historical and geographical picture.

In 1849, or earlier, the vineyards in San Benito County now known as Valliant Vineyards were started by Theophile Vaché. In Santa Clara, Almadén, Paul Masson and Martin Ray are the successors to wine making traditions begun in 1852. In the same county Mirassou Vineyards originated a year later, some four years earlier than Buena Vista in Sonoma. The early sixties saw the beginnings of Charles Krug in Napa and of Schramsberg. Dating back to the seventies are Beringer Brothers in Napa, and Inglenook in Napa.

In the eighties a galaxy of famous wineries was founded, including Italian Swiss Colony and Korbel in Sonoma, Mt. La Salle (The Christian Brothers) in Napa, Brookside Vineyard Company of Guasti, Cresta Blanca, Wente and Concannon in Alameda, Italian Vineyards Company (I.V.C.) in San Bernardino (now owned by the Guild Wine Company), California Wine Association in San Francisco, Digardi in Contra Costa, Petri in San Joaquin, Ruby Hill in Alameda, the Novitiate of Los Gatos in Santa Clara and Bisceglia Brothers in Fresno.

The nineties witnessed the foundings of Roma, now of Fresno, of

San Martin in Santa Clara and of Foppiano, in Sonoma. In 1900 the foundations were laid for Beaulieu in Napa.

Since then many other wineries, great and small, have risen to establish noteworthy wine making traditions of their own.

Prohibition dealt a severe blow to American viticulture in general and that of California in particular. It was a senseless attack, as Prohibition has never led the way to moderation and encroaches deeply on man's freedom of judgment. A substantial part of California's vineyard acreage was maintained for the production of wines for sacramental and medicinal purposes and for supplying grapes to home wine makers, as allowed by the dry laws. Other vineyards were turned over to the cultivation of table grapes and to the manufacture of grape juice.

After Repeal the California wine industry was rebuilt on a sound basis with the State Department of Public Health and the federal government becoming joint guardians for the maintenance of standards as to the identity and labeling of wines.

California is responsible for roughly 80 per cent of the wine produced in the United States, and for about 75 per cent of that consumed in this country. Ten years ago, 75 per cent of California's production consisted of aperitif and dessert wines, compared with only slightly more than half today. The balance is mainly table and sparkling or carbonated wines. Although exact figures are hard to come by, it has been estimated that about four-fifths of California table wines are red (including rosés), and about one-fifth white.

The climate and soil of California are particularly well suited to the vines of the *Vitis vinifera* family. Beginning with the days of Jean Louis Vignes and of Agoston Haraszthy, practically every variety of these vines has been planted in California, many of them with great success. By the alchemy of local conditions they yield wines which often differ in character from those produced in their original environments. California wines, while often similar or identical in name to European types, should always be considered on their own merits, but comparisons, it seems, are often inevitable.

The same grapes also develop differently in the various regions and climates of California. Maturity is slow in cooler areas. White grapes retain more acid and develop less sweetness, while dark grapes attain the maximum coloring matter in their skins. These regions are best suited for the production of dry table wines and of sparkling wines of quality. Under warmer conditions grapes develop less acid and a greater sugar content. Such zones are better adapted to the production of dessert wines.

It is known exactly to which localities each grape variety is best suited or whether its cultivation should be avoided altogether. Such studies and recommendations are among the important functions of the Department of Viticulture and Enology of the University of California's College of Agriculture at Davis in Yolo County and of a similar department at Fresno State College.

Full recognition must be given to a great line of university figures who have wisely guided California's viticulture and are seeking constant improvement. First of that line was the famed Dean Hilgard who was succeeded by Bioletti, or the great Bioletti as he is often referred to. Both have long since passed on, to supervise, it may be hoped, the heavenly vineyards. Their places were taken by such men, professors of viticulture or enology, as Winkler, Amerine, Olmo, Singleton, Berg, Guymon, Kunkee, Webb, Cook, Lider, Weaver, Kliewer, Nelson and the late W. V. Cruess, familiar figures to all members of the wine industry.

Other researchers, best known among them Dr. Salvatore Lucia, Professor Emeritus of Preventive Medicine at the University of California Medical Center in San Francisco, have rediscovered wine's nutritional and medicinal benefits. They have learned that it is a complex food, useful as a dietary supplement or tranquilizer for patients afflicted with a variety of ailments.

Wine growing and wine production are important and fundamental parts of California's agriculture. There are many more farmer-growers than producers. The interests of both should be adequately protected. Wine making is also a business, subject to the hazards of weather and diseases, to fluctuating grape prices, and to high labor costs. It is at the same time an art, requiring the skill, patience, and devotion of experts.

Fine wines are produced from the better wine grapes, but the latter are often sparse yielders. Standard wines are the product of the more heavily yielding vines of lesser quality. Inferior wines are not infrequently made with table grapes.

Wines produced from the finest grapes naturally will command a higher price. For such wines the name on the label of an outstanding wine grower is helpful as a guarantee of quality. If a sound standard quality wine is sought at a lower price, then the name of a volume producer of a nationally distributed brand should be looked for. These wines are advertised widely and provide good value for the money.

California wine growers often produce, bottle and market wines of many different types, growing some grapes themselves and buying the rest from growers in the neighborhood or from other districts. It is customary for a large producer to market a variety of table wines as well as aperitif and dessert wines and often sparkling wines as well. One reason for this custom is that many different varieties of grapes flourish in the same vicinity; vines which are strangers or even rivals in Europe become friendly neighbors in California. Another, and very potent, reason is that it is much more profitable to market a large variety of wines than otherwise. Only a few California wineries produce wines only from grapes grown in their own vineyards. Most of them buy outside grapes as needed and many bottle wines they do not produce themselves in order to complete the selection of wines they want to market. It must be stressed that the fact that a wine is actually produced at a specific winery from homegrown grapes only can never be as important as the quality of the wine itself, backed by the reputation of the winery which either produces or markets it.

Part One

I

CALIFORNIA TABLE WINES

*T*HE TABLE WINES of California can best be classified according to color; red, white or rosé, and as to whether they are *generic* or *varietal*.

By *generic* is meant a wine called after its European prototype which it resembles, more or less. The names are familiar, easy to pronounce and are met with the world over. In California the best known of such table wines are burgundy, claret and chianti in the reds, sauterne, chablis and rhine in the whites, and vin rosé meaning pink wine.

By *varietal* is meant a wine named after a particular *variety of grape,* from which it is principally or exclusively produced and having the easily recognizable taste characteristics of the variety. The best known California varietal red table wines are Cabernet Sauvignon, Zinfandel, Pinot Noir and Gamay. In the whites they are: Sauvignon Blanc and Semillon; Chardonnay, Pinot Blanc and Chenin Blanc; White Riesling, Traminer, Sylvaner and Grey Riesling. In the rosés they are Grenache Rosé, Gamay Rosé and Cabernet Rosé. These are all names to remember if one wishes to serve the more distinctive and finer table wines of California.

In marketing a table wine with a generic name the producer either tries to approximate the European wine type after which it is called or he simply uses the name in response to public demand. The public insists on burgundy and sauterne. The producers, to stay in business, must comply.

The trend towards varietal table wines is increasing as the public becomes more particular as to quality and flavor. The laws are strict and a wine can—or should be—called after a grape *only* if 51% or more of the wine is produced from the grape. A varietal wine should also possess the distinctive color, aroma and flavor of the particular grape. These qualities should be easily recognizable and not only by the experts. There is little point in producing a varietal wine just for the sake of the name.

Some fine California table wines are produced from a careful blending of choice grape varieties, each lending its own character to the final product. The French Bordeaux wines, both red and white, are usually blended in this manner. There is a place in California for blends as well as for the varietals, straight or otherwise.

Vintage years matter less in California than in France and Germany where temperatures, affecting the grape harvests and the resulting wines, vary considerably. Even so, some years in California are more favorable than others and there is a definite trend towards marketing the table wines of exceptionally fine vintages at a higher price. This development must be warmly welcomed as is the tendency towards differentiating between superior table wines that mature in different vats. There is that elusive quality in nature that seeks perfection in all things.

Indication of the vintage on a California wine also serves to identify it to the consumer. Vintage charts would only be of real value if made up by each winery for each type of wine produced, indicating the vineyards of origin. Incidentally, if a vintage is mentioned on the label, the wine must, by law, have been produced 100% in the year indicated.

Which are the finest California table wines?

The answer involves three separate factors: the grapes from which the wines are made, the district of origin, and the reputation of the wine grower.

The best table wine grapes yield the finest wines. It is therefore useful to be familiar with these grapes after which the finer varietals are named.

The superior table wine grapes flourish the best in the cooler climatic zones, where they grow and mature "the hard way." For that reason the finest California table wines hail from the northern coastal counties, notably in the counties or valleys of *Napa, Sonoma, Livermore, Santa Clara, Santa Cruz, San Benito* and *Monterey.*

These are the "appellations of origin" to look for on the label when desiring the best. Any such appellation means, by law, that the wine has been produced from grapes grown and fermented at least 75% in the area designated.

Premium table wines are also produced in other northern sections as in the counties of Mendocino, Solano and Contra Costa. There has been a resurgence of winegrowing in the Mother Lode counties of the Sierra foothills.

Separate mention must be made of the red table wines produced in the Cucamonga district of San Bernardino County in Southern California. Many of these wines carry the *Cucamonga* appellation of origin on the label.

The ultimate guarantee of quality for any wine is the reputation of the grower or producer.

CHART OF THE MORE PROMINENT CALIFORNIA RED TABLE WINES

Varietals	Generics
CABERNET SAUVIGNON	Claret
PINOT NOIR	Burgundy
GAMAY	
ZINFANDEL	
BARBERA	Chianti
GRIGNOLINO	Vino Rosso
PETITE SIRAH	

II

CALIFORNIA RED TABLE WINES

A. Varietals

CABERNET SAUVIGNON (Ca-berr-nay' So-vee-nyon')

*C*HE CABERNET SAUVIGNON, to use its full and proper name, is the premier claret grape of the world. It is mainly responsible for the superb character and flavor of the celebrated château-bottled and other clarets of the Bordeaux region in France.

In California the Cabernet Sauvignon grape can yield, in the northern coastal region, altogether superior wines. Napa, Santa Clara, Santa Cruz and Sonoma counties produce the finest, some of which are great wines anywhere under the sun.

The finest Cabernet Sauvignons are produced from considerably more than the legal minimum of 51% of grapes of that name as the wine will not stand much blending without loss of character. The best have a deep ruby color, an expansive bouquet and a remarkable flavor, easy to recognize and appreciate. When young they possess a dryness and aromatic pungency that smooth out with age to a rich mellowness. A common mistake is to serve them at a temperature cooler than the average room. At room temperature their inherent tartness will dissolve into their rightful soft and mellow flavor.

There is a wide range of Cabernet Sauvignons, depending on the location of the vineyard, the grower, the age, and even the vat in which the wine matured.

When one desires the best "claret type" California can produce, a fine Cabernet Sauvignon is the wine to buy.

CABERNET

A wine, labeled simply Cabernet, can be one of very different things and the term is therefore confusing.

It could be made mainly of Cabernet Sauvignon grapes (see above) and should then properly so have been named.

It could be made principally from the Ruby Cabernet grape (see below) in which case it would better have been labeled by its own name.

It could be made from a blend of various grapes with the Cabernet name. The label may tell the story or it may not.

This writer, for one, is for abolishing the term entirely.

RUBY CABERNET

A fairly new varietal in the red table wine field. Propagated by the Agricultural Experiment Station of the University of California, the vine is a hybrid of the Cabernet Sauvignon and of the Carignane grapes from a cross made in 1936 which first fruited in 1940. Purpose of the cross was to combine the outstanding character of the Cabernet Sauvignon with the productivity of the Carignane in an attempt to combine high quality and yielding ability in the same variety.

The color of Ruby Cabernet is the same as that of its august parent, Cabernet Sauvignon. Its aroma and flavor, though similar, are much less distinguished.

Ruby Cabernet rates as a red table wine of higher than average quality. The wine is varietally produced in a number of northern coastal and San Joaquin Valley counties.

ZINFANDEL

The leading red wine grape of California in acreage, production and originality.

Its origin is uncertain. The best known theory was that the wine was first imported to California by Colonel Agoston Haraszthy, who planted these vines at his Buena Vista estate near Sonoma where they flourished and made viticultural history.

Zinfandel varies considerably in quality and character, the best coming from the coastal counties. It can be a wine of peculiar charm, fruity, zestful and aromatic with a raspberry like flavor. It is essentially Californian in type and has the great advantage of being remarkably inexpensive.

If price conscious and still wanting a varietal red table wine, a good Zinfandel is the wine to look for.

PINOT NOIR (Pee′-no Nwahr)

This is the famous grape that yields the finest of the Red Burgundies of France and the "Blanc de noir" wines from which most of the unblended French Champagnes are produced.

In California the Pinot noir grape* produces wines that can be superb in aroma and flavor, harmonious, soft, smooth and velvety. One hundred % Pinot Noir in California is almost always light in color as the grape does not carry much pigment so blending to darken color is nearly standard practice.

Napa, Santa Clara and Sonoma counties originate the best. The vine, however, is difficult to cultivate and the wine itself is as difficult to produce properly. Availability of the true Pinot Noir wine is limited and wine, so labeled, varies greatly in quality. It can never be cheap if genuine.

If one desires the highest quality California red burgundy type then a truly fine Pinot Noir is the wine to purchase.

GAMAY BEAUJOLAIS (Ga-may′ Bo-zho-lay′) and GAMAY

The Gamay is the grape that made the Beaujolais wines of France famous and is responsible for their gay and fruity character.

---

* Pinot Noir is the correct spelling for the *wine* and Pinot noir for the *grape*. This principle applies to all wines and grapes where the name is followed by an adjective.

In California the Gamay produces a light colored, lively and fruity wine with a delicate flavor.

There are many varieties of the Gamay vine, all similar, more or less. Gamay Beaujolais is produced in Santa Clara and San Benito Counties, while the Napa County variety is always labeled simply as Gamay.

It may be noted that Gamay, like Beaujolais in France, is often served at cellar temperature.

RED PINOT (Pinot St. George)

There is no grape by the name of Red Pinot. The term, however, has won limited acceptance as a red table wine, produced from the Pinot St. George grape, the name under which the wine itself should also be known.

Pinot St. George, no relation to the pinot family but a variety from the south of France, produces a wine of its own distinctive charm, soft, fruity and fragrant. It is produced only in the Napa Valley.

PETITE SIRAH (Pet-eet Sear-ah)

An ancient *vinifera* grape, said to have been brought by the Crusaders from the Middle East to the Rhone Valley of France, where it produces the red wines of Hermitage. It was transplanted to California and is widely grown. A few wineries such as Concannon Vineyards in Livermore bottle Petite Sirah as red varietal, although most use it as a blending wine.

BARBERA

A native of Piedmont, Italy, which has done very well in California. The grape yields a big, rugged, fullbodied, richly colored and very pleasant wine with plenty of flavor and tang which yet can be quite soft to the palate. It is characterized by high acidity which it retains very well. Notable Barberas are produced in Sonoma, Italy and Alameda counties.

GRIGNOLINO

Another native of Piedmont producing in California a wine with an original and popular appeal. Its fragrant bouquet is said to remind one of strawberries and its orange-red color is typical and unique. It is sometimes bottled, on account of its light color, as Grignolino Rosé. The best known Grignolinos are produced in Cucamonga and in Napa.

Charbono

Also said to originate in Piedmont, this grape produces a deep-colored, soft and heavy bodied wine.

Calzin

A red grape introduced in 1958 by the University of California.

Royalty and Rubired

Two red varieties developed at Davis by University of California scientists. Both have high color and are useful as blending wines or for making California port. At least one winery has begun marketing Royalty as a varietal table wine.

B. Generics

RED TABLE WINE

A wine which has become increasingly popular and is often of very good quality, selling in the medium price range. It makes no pretenses and can be produced from a wide variety of grapes. It seems to be taking the place of Claret and is usually of better quality than the latter.

CLARET

Usually a standard quality wine of no particular distinction, although there are exceptions. Claret used to mean any acceptable red table wine, resembling Red Bourdeaux more or less and usually less. The term seems to be headed for extinction, its place being taken by Red Table Wine (see above) or Burgundy (see below).

BURGUNDY

The most common appellation today for a generic table wine of no particular varietal distinction. It can be pleasant enough and has superseded what once used to be sold as Claret. The public demands Burgundy and gets it.

California wine, labeled Burgundy, varies greatly in quality, and ranges from poor to very good indeed, notably when produced by the better known growers of the northern coastal counties.

CHIANTI

The wine of this name is usually marketed in raffia or straw-covered, bulb shaped bottles. In California Chianti has become a type of wine, ruby red, fruity, earthy, medium tart and rather full-bodied, the best known of which is produced in Asti, Sonoma County.

Note: The four generics described above actually overlap in color, body and other characteristics, the main differences often being the bottle shapes.

VINO ROSSO

This type of table wine, mellow and slightly sweet, is similar to the homemade table wines produced by many people of Italian origin throughout the country. The commercial wine of this type, quite inexpensive, has won wide acceptance, especially in Italian circles. Many growers produce it, labeling it with various Italian names. The original dryness in the wine is often compensated by the addition of a slight amount of port.

CHART OF THE MORE PROMINENT CALIFORNIA WHITE TABLE WINES

Varietals	Generics
SEMILLON SAUVIGNON BLANC	Sauterne
CHARDONNAY PINOT BLANC CHENIN BLANC FOLLE BLANCHE	Chablis
WHITE RIESLING (JOHANNISBERG) TRAMINER SYLVANER GREY RIESLING	Riesling Rhine Wine Moselle

III

CALIFORNIA WHITE TABLE WINES

A. VARIETALS

SEMILLON (Sem-me-yon′)

*O*NE OF the finest white wine grapes in the world and responsible, together with the Sauvignon Blanc (see below), for the
character of the famous Sauternes and Graves wines of France.

Semillon, when produced by a top flight grower in one of the
northern coastal counties, ranks as one of the finest California wines
of the Sauternes type. It is golden, medium to fullbodied with a rich
flavor and a flowery bouquet and ranges from dry to sweet.

Outstanding Semillon wines are produced in the Livermore Valley
and other very good ones originate in Napa and Santa Clara.

SAUVIGNON BLANC (So′-vee-nyon Blon)

The principal grape variety used for the production of the white
Graves wine of Bordeaux and also important in that of the French
Sauternes. Known in France as the Sauvignon, it is called Sauvignon
blanc in California to distinguish it clearly from the Sauvignon vert
(see below).

Sauvignon Blanc is a high quality wine with a distinctive aromatic character, fuller in body and heavier than Semillon. Like the latter it ranges from dry to sweet, the best hailing from the Livermore Valley with its gravelly soil.

Sauvignon Vert (So'-vee-nyon Vair)

The grape is widely cultivated and much used in blending and in the production of California Sauterne of average quality.

It is occasionally met with bottled as a varietal type and can be quite pleasing with its dry character and slight muscat flavor.

French Colombard

Another vigorous producer yielding a wine with a high acid content useful for blending in California chablis and rhine wine types. As a varietal wine it is dry, light, tart, pale golden with a neutral flavor.

CHARDONNAY or PINOT CHARDONNAY
(Pee'-no Shar-don-nay)

One of the greatest white wine grapes of all but a sparse yielder. It is celebrated for producing the finest white burgundies and Chablis of France as well as being used for French Champagne.

In the cooler northern coastal counties the grape can yield a distinguished wine, golden, fullbodied and fragrant, flavorful and smooth, reminiscent of still champagne.

The wine is known under both names indicated above which is confusing and incorrect. It is hoped the first term, which is the right one, will be agreed upon.

When the finest California wine of the white burgundy or chablis type is the object, this is the wine to secure, bottled by an outstanding grower.

PINOT BLANC (Pee'-no Blon)

A grape second only to the Chardonnay in the white burgundy class. It has made an enviable reputation for itself in California where it can yield an elegant wine of distinctive aroma and flavor, smooth and dry, fresh and fruity. Like Chardonnay its favorite California homes are in the Livermore, Napa and Santa Clara valleys.

Some Pinot Blanc is labeled Pinot Blanc Vrai or True Pinot Blanc. This seems unnecessary as the wine is a Pinot Blanc or it isn't. If it isn't, it should be labeled differently.

White Pinot

A misnomer as there is no grape by that name and a very confusing term which, it is hoped, is headed for extinction.

Literally, it is of course the translation of Pinot Blanc but if a wine is made from Pinot blanc grapes it should naturally be labeled as Pinot Blanc (see above).

Actually the term won wide acceptance at one time, and still unfortunately does, for a wine, good enough in its own right, made from the Chenin blanc grape (see below).

CHENIN BLANC (She-nin Blon)

A wine made from the Chenin blanc or Pineau de la Loire grape famous in France for the white wines of Anjou and Touraine of which the delightful Vouvray is the best known.

In California the Chenin blanc grape has done very well also, notably in Napa County, where it produces a very pleasing light and fruity wine, that varies from dry to quite sweet.

The modern tendency is to bottle the wine under its rightful name, Chenin Blanc. Occasionally it is still marketed as White Pinot (see above).

FOLLE BLANCHE (Fol Blonsh)

The grape is one of the principal varieties grown in the Charente district in France for the distillation of cognac. Transplanted to California it has become a much better drinking wine than in its native soil.

The wine has a rather high acid content making it useful for the production of champagne and the better grades of California chablis. It is occasionally met with as a varietal type, notably from the Napa

Valley hillsides and is tartly dry, fresh and fruity, clean both to the nose and palate. A nice, light, luncheon wine.

GREEN HUNGARIAN

The origin of the vine is obscure but is said, as the name implies, to originate in Hungry. It yields a dry wine mostly used in blending. It is, however, varietally produced, hailing from Napa, Alameda and Sonoma counties and yielding wines that are quite different in character but with their own individual charm. They are at their best when not served too cold.

WHITE RIESLING or JOHANNISBERG RIESLING
(Rees'-ling)

A premier white wine grape called Riesling in Germany where it is responsible for all the great Rhines and Moselles. It is also extensively cultivated in Alsace, Switzerland, California and elsewhere.

In California the grape is called White Riesling to distinguish it clearly from other varieties with a Riesling name such as Sylvaner or Franken Riesling, Grey Riesling and Emerald Riesling (see below under those names). Properly, the wine should be called White Riesling and is sometimes so labeled but to the confusion of retailers, restaurants and the public many growers label this wine Johannisberg Riesling naming it after some of the finest of all Riesling wines, those produced by Fürst (Prince) von Metternich at Schloss Johannisberg in the Rheingau district of Germany. This custom seems presumptuous as the correct name of White Riesling renders sufficient honor to one of California's truly great wines while trespassing on no foreign glory. Some producers market this wine with the even longer name of Johannisberger Reisling but federal regulations, thank goodness, frown on this practice and the term is bound to disappear in the near future.

White (or Johannisberg) Riesling is a most refreshing wine, with a pronounced fragrance of bouquet and a rich, satisfying flavor. Napa, Santa Clara, Santa Cruz and San Benito counties are best known for its production. Depending on the vineyard, some are lighter, delicate and pale green, others are fuller in body, fruitier and dark golden.

TRAMINER (Tra-mee'-ner) or GEWURZTRAMINER (Ge-wurts-tra-mee'-ner)

Two names for the same grape, famed in Alsace, France, and known in California as the Red Traminer on account of the red flush on its skin when ripening. The term Gewurztraminer is sometimes also used to denote selected strains of the Traminer grape.

The wines are fragrant and distinctly aromatic with a spicy scent and flavor and are generally rated as the finest rhine wine types of California after the White Rieslings. They are produced in Napa, Santa Clara and Sonoma counties.

Flora

A white, aromatic, Traminer-type variety introduced in 1958 by the University of California.

SYLVANER or Franken Riesling

The principal rhine wine type grape grown in California. It is known as the Sylvaner in Alsace, France and as the Franken Riesling in some parts of Germany. In California it is known under both names, but more correctly under that of Sylvaner.

The wines are of superior quality, fragrant and fresh with a delicate aroma and flavor. It is bottled as a varietal in Napa, Santa Clara and Sonoma counties, usually under the Sylvaner name but sometimes, presumably to take advantage of the Riesling name but leading to unnecessary confusion, as plain Riesling (see below under the white generics).

GREY RIESLING

The grape, actually the Chauché gris of France and not a Riesling at all, yields in California a soft and pleasing wine with a mild and spicy flavor. It has attained great popularity and the demand often exceeds the supply. The best known Grey Riesling comes from the Livermore Valley but it is also produced in Napa, Santa Clara and Cucamonga.

EMERALD RIESLING

A hybrid of the White Riesling and the Muscadelle, originated by the University of California at Davis.

The wine rates as a table wine of above average quality and has a clean, fresh, tart taste. It spoils easily, however, acquiring a brown color and an oxidized flavor.

Helena

Another University of California-developed grape variety. Its characteristics include a high acid content.

Veltliner (Velt'-leener)

The Red Veltliner grapes can produce an agreeable white wine, somewhat similar to Traminer (see above). The grapes have a slight pink blush when ripe which explains their name.

The wine has sufficient varietal character to warrant bottling as such. Much wine bottled as Traminer (see above) actually comes from Veltliner grapes as the two are often confused in the vineyards.

Malvasia Bianca (White Malvasia)

The grape is a muscat flavored variety of the Malvasia vines which are said to originate in Greece and are widely grown in Europe. In California it yields a sweet light table wine of delicate bouquet and flavor. It is variously labeled by its full and correct name of Malvasia Bianca and as California Malvasia without indication of color.

The wine should not be confused with the dessert wine of the same name (see page 46) nor with the scarce red Malvasia table and dessert wines.

Gold

A variety introduced primarily as a table grape, but one which produces also a light, sweet table wine.

B. Generics

WHITE TABLE WINE

Unassumingly named, California White Table Wine varies from average to very good indeed. It is usually dry. Many white wines, sold under fancier names, regional and other, would do as well if not better were they labeled with this simple and straightforward appellation. It is a matter of educating the public.

SAUTERNE(S), Dry, Medium and Sweet

California Sauterne is usually spelled without the final "s" of French Sauternes. A few growers use the French spelling but the general tendency is to the shorter, Americanized form.

Sauterne is produced in California from a variety of grapes, from the finest to the prolific but neutral tasting Thompson Seedless, which is actually a table grape. It ranges from dry to sweet, from straw to golden in color, while its bouquet and flavor depend on the grapes used.

Hautee Sauterne has come to mean a sweet or medium sweet California Sauterne while Chateau Sauterne is reserved for the sweetest type, often made from Semillon and/or Sauvignon blanc grapes, with the addition sometimes of a little Muscadelle, the same grapes from which the best French Sauternes are also produced.

The finest California wines of the Sauternes type, outside of the Chateau wines just mentioned, are the varietal wines known as Semillon and Sauvignon Blanc (see under white varietals).

CHABLIS (Sha-blee′)

The generic type of white burgundy named after the famed French wines of that name from the Chablis region.

California Chablis is pale in color, usually more delicate than sauterne, and less tart than rhine wine. It is made from a variety of
grapes, from fine to indifferent.

Some excellent chablis is produced in the northern coastal counties
by outstanding growers. The inexpensive ones are often not to be
distinguished from dry sauterne and rhine wines of the same brand.

Rhine Wine

The California wine so labeled is made from a variety of grapes
and often from the same as those from which chablis (see above) is
derived but blended in such a manner that a paler, drier and tarter
wine is obtained.

The best of these wines are the product of one or more of the Riesling grapes (see below) and then possess the aroma, flavor and
character of the latter.

Riesling (Rees'-ling)

This wine can be a number of varietals or a blend of some or of all
of them. The term has become confusing and in this writer's opinion
had better be abolished altogether.

If the wine is a true varietal, made from 51% or more from either
the White (Johannisberg) Riesling, the Sylvaner (Franken Riesling), the Grey Riesling or the Emerald Riesling (see under the
varietal whites) it should be labeled under one of those names.

It can also be a blend of one or more of these wines without any of
them predominating. The result is that California Riesling varies
greatly in character and quality, depending on the grapes used, the
district or vineyard of origin and the grower. It has, in fact, become a
meaningless appellation.

Note: Riesling is often misspelled and mispronounced "Reisling,"
presumably because of an erroneous impression that it sounds more
Germanic.

Moselle

This term used to be popular to designate California wine of the Rhine type. It is still occasionally used for table wines but is more familiar in describing sparkling white wines that have been carbonated.

White Chianti

This wine is marketed, like its much more popular red counterpart (see Chianti under the red generics), in raffia or straw-covered bulb-shaped bottles. Its production is very limited.

Vino Bianco

A mellow and sweetish white wine, the counterpart of Vino Rosso (see there) and labeled under different Italian names.

Light Muscat

A light wine, produced from muscat grapes, and varying from sweet to very sweet. It is sometimes labeled as California Light Sweet Wine.

Dry Muscat

A dry white wine made from muscat grapes with limited appeal.

May Wine

A white wine, flavored with waldmeister (woodruff) quite popular in Germany, especially in spring time, where it is served cold, in a bowl, with fruit in season. In California it is produced in several areas and should be better known.

Retsina

A wine of Greek origin, produced in California to a very limited extent and possessing a tang, appealing particularly to those of Greek extraction. The special flavor is due to the addition of resin (retsina).

CHART OF THE MORE PROMINENT
ROSÉ (PINK) TABLE WINES

Varietals	Generics
GRENACHE ROSÉ GAMAY ROSÉ Cabernet Rosé Zinfandel Rosé Grignolino Rosé Pinot Noir Rosé (a rarity)	Vin Rosé (Pink Wine) Rosé

IV

CALIFORNIA ROSÉ (PINK) TABLE WINES

A. Varietals

GRENACHE ROSÉ (Gre-nash' Ro-zay)

*T*HE GRENACHE is the grape mainly responsible for the well known French rosé wines from the Tavel district in the Valley of the Rhône.

In California the Grenache is best suited to the coolest regions of the northern coastal counties where it yields one of the most typical and best rosé wines of the state. Both dry and semi-sweet types are produced, the former being the finer.

GAMAY ROSÉ

Made from one of the varieties of the Gamay grape, this is an excellent wine, hailing notably from the Napa and Livermore Valleys. It is usually bottled as a varietal but is sometimes labeled simply as Rosé or Vin Rosé (see below under the Generics) or with some special proprietary name dreamed up by the grower.

Cabernet Rosé

The Cabernet Sauvignon grape yields a very good rosé table wine, bottled sometimes under the varietal name and sometimes under a proprietary label of the grower.

Zinfandel Rosé

Zinfandel is another grape that lends itself well to the production of rosés with a distinctive bouquet and flavor.

Grignolino Rosé

The Grignolino grape yields a light colored red wine in the first place and so with little effort a rosé can be produced from it. It is produced both in the Napa Valley and in the Cucamonga district.

Pinot Noir Rosé

A rare and choice rosé with distinctive character and flavor.

B. GENERICS

Vin Rosé (Pink Wine) or Rosé

Wines so labeled are produced from a variety of grapes including those used for the varietals (see above). Lesser grades are simply blends of red and white wines.

While the best and more typical rosé wines are dry, fruity and slightly but pleasantly tart, quite a few are on the sweeter side, containing a certain amount of residual sugar. Some are even quite sweet.

V

TABLE WINES PLUS

*U*NDER REGULATIONS that went into effect July first 1959 it became permissible to market table wines containing up to 5 lbs per square inch pressure of carbon dioxide, defining in effect by law the point at which still wines are separated from sparkling wines. Actually wines containing not more than 5 lbs carbon dioxide are not effervescent. It simply allows growers to produce wines under a blanket of carbon dioxide at lower temperatures thereby obtaining more fresh, fruity flavored wines.

"Legally they can not be differentiated from their counterparts which do not contain carbon dioxide" the magazine *Wines and Vines* said; "the label can not state or even intimate that there is some carbon dioxide in the wine; nor can the wine be advertised as containing this gas. Furthermore the brand name is not supposed to give any clue to the fact that the wine has some carbon dioxide . . ."

A good many of these wines have been marketed by companies such as Gallo, United Vintners and Guild, and one or more brands of each of the three firms contains appreciable Vitis labrusca (Concord) to give an "American" or "foxy" flavor. In this, the winemakers probably took their cue from the new rage for Cold Duck sparkling wine.

CHART OF THE MORE PROMINENT
CALIFORNIA SPARKLING WINES

Varietals	Sparkling Wine Type	
Pinot Noir Chardonnay	Champagne *Nature* *Brut* *Extra Dry* *Sec* or *Dry* *Demi Sec* *Doux* or *Sweet*	really dry fairly dry medium dry to rather sweet really sweet
	Pink Champagne or Champagne Rosé	medium dry to sweet
	Red Champagne and Sparkling Burgundy	on the dry side on the sweet side
	Sparkling Muscat or Moscato Spumante Moscato Amabile	definitely sweet
	Cold Duck	sweet

VI

CALIFORNIA SPARKLING WINES

*T*HE BEST California champagnes and other sparkling wines are produced according to the French champagne method whereby the secondary fermentation which causes the sparkle takes place in the very bottle containing the wine eventually sold to the consumer. They include California champagne from very dry to sweet, California pink or Rosé Champagne and California Red Champagne.

The same wines are produced by the faster and less costly method whereby the secondary fermentation occurs in glass lined tanks or vats according to the so-called bulk or Charmat process. The law requires that sparkling wines produced in this manner be designated as "bulk process" on the label.

In both methods discussed above the wines have been fermented naturally to obtain their sparkle. So when the term "naturally fermented" appears on the labeling this only means that their sparkle has not been obtained by artificial means. Wines where the sparkle has been induced by artificial means are known as Carbonated or Effervescent wines cannot be labeled as "Sparkling."

A new technique for carbonating wine invented by F. Justin Miller of Rutherford in Napa County has sparked a great deal of interest. Its main advantage lies in the fact that most artificially charged wines tend to lose their sparkle rapidly, while "Millerway" wines retain theirs even longer than those produced by natural fermentation. At least one premium winery has adopted the process.

All sparkling wines are expensive due to the high federal tax which is twenty times that on table or still wines, taxing in effect, not so much the wine as the bubbles.

Champagne

The finest California bottle fermented champagnes and other sparkling wines come from the northern coastal counties. Fair ones are produced in Southern California's Cucamonga district. Bulk fermented champagnes of quality are made in these districts as well as in the Great Inland Valley Region.

Pinot noir and Chardonnay, the grapes used to make the great French champagnes, yield the finest California champagnes but other grapes do very well also, such as Semillon, White Riesling, Sylvaner, Folle blanche, and Chenin blanc.

Some, if little, varietal champagne is marketed, indicating on the labeling that it was made from either Pinot noir or Chardonnay grapes.

In California, as elsewhere, a so-called *dosage* or liqueuring is added to the finished wine before inserting the final cork. This *dosage* consists of brandy, wine and sugar, the amount depending on the degree of dryness or sweetness the producer desires to give to his product.

Now it is a peculiar fact that people often like to fool themselves and so it is with champagne. They like to *think* they like a dry champagne but actually they prefer it to be not so dry. That explains why a champagne labeled *Brut* which is, or was, supposed to be very dry indeed, may not be so very dry at all. An *Extra Dry* champagne is a contradiction, in itself, for it is often not "dry" at all while champagnes labeled "Sec" or "Dry" are usually on the sweet side! This system works out to satisfaction of both producer and consumer.

The driest type of champagne made, and only to a very small extent in California, is *Nature,* with no dosage added at all. This type is really dry, though if properly made, not harsh or acid, just right. It is also the most difficult to produce.

Brut champagne is the next driest and very popular with "gourmets" and "connoisseurs" who will order no other unless it were the *Nature*. *Extra Dry* is a happy medium that will satisfy most champagne lovers while *Sec* or *Dry*, *Demi Sec* and *Doux* or *Sweet* lean progressively more to the sweet side and are dessert wines.

The dosage used in the various types will differ slightly according to the producer. Some do not indicate at all on the label what degree of dryness or sweetness their wine possesses. In such cases it is safe to assume that the champagne is in the medium range.

Pink Champagne or Champagne Rosé

A pink sparkling wine, either bottle fermented or produced in bulk fermentation. It is pretty to look at and favored by the ladies. The designation "Oeil de Perdrix" or "Partridge Eye" has sometimes been accorded this wine in California. In France the term refers to the pink tinge champagne sometimes acquires when made exclusively from dark grapes. California champagne made from Pinot noir grapes only will often have this pink hue.

Red Champagne or Champagne Rouge

A name dreamed up by growers who felt that a high quality *bottle fermented* sparkling wine should have a name other than "Sparkling Burgundy" (see below) as the latter is not required by law to indicate on the label whether it is bottle or bulk fermented.

Sparkling Burgundy

Very popular and very pretty. It is produced from a variety of grapes, is rarely bottle fermented and always on the sweet side.

Sparkling Muscat or Moscato Spumante

A sweet sparkling wine with a distinctive muscat aroma and flavor, usually produced from the Muscat of Alexandria grape.

For the Italian trade this wine is often marketed as Moscato Spumante or Gran Spumante, names reminiscent of Italy's best known sparkling wine, Asti Spumante.

Moscato Amabile

An effervescent wine, light in alcohol and very delicate, produced in the Napa Valley. The Italian word *amabile* is used to indicate, as in Italy, that the wine is sweet.

Moscato Amabile, owing to its low degree of alcohol, does not "travel well," losing its sparkle easily. It should be kept in the refrigerator and consumed soon after purchase.

Sparkling Malvasia

Made from the Malvasia bianca grape this wine has a delicate muscat character and is on the sweet side.

Cold Duck

We are at a loss to explain fully the popularity of this concoction, but then we didn't understand why Americans began drinking straight gin instead of martinis either.

Cold Duck apparently takes its name from *Kalte Ente,* a German punch made by mixing red or white table wine with *Sekt,* the German version of Champagne. Other ingredients such as lemon, sugar and brandy helped disguise the bad wines of poor vintage years.

The American Cold Duck originally came from Michigan and had a heavy flavor of Concord grapes. As the fad for so-called "pop wines" swept the country, Cold Duck began to appear in California, some containing Concord, some simple combinations of red and white sparkling wines.

Cold Duck is generally sweet and should be well chilled.

CHART OF THE MORE PROMINENT CALIFORNIA APERITIF AND DESSERT WINES

Varietals	Generics
Palomino	Sherry (*flor* and regular): Pale Dry and Cocktail (dry) Golden (medium) Cream (sweet)
Tinta Madeira	Port Ruby Port Tawny Port Vintage Port
Muscat Frontignan Aleatico	Muscatel (mostly from Muscat of Alexandria) Black Muscat
	Dry Vermouth Light Dry Vermouth Sweet Vermouth
	Marsala Madeira

VII

CALIFORNIA APERITIF
AND DESSERT WINES

$\mathcal{T}$HESE WINES constitute about half of California's wine production. They are sometimes called "dessert wines" and although most of them have a relatively high sugar content there are "dry" types among them as well as all the variations between "dry" and "sweet." In this *Guide* they are grouped together as "Aperitif and Dessert Wines" for the simple reason that even the sweet types are often used as aperitifs before the meal. In fact, in the United States, the term "dessert wine" is really a complete misnomer as very few people actually serve the sweet types with the dessert. They are used between meals, as an evening refreshment or in the afternoon or morning with or without cookies or cake. Or, as stated above, as aperitif wines before the meal. It is nonsense, in this writer's opinion, to ban a sweet sherry or port, or even a muscat, before the meal as an aperitif. Many women, and even men will enjoy such a wine before the meal. Such has been, and still is the custom in many lands of the world. It is only a British custom that Port is traditionally *never* served before the dessert.

Aperitif and dessert wines used to contain about 20% alcohol per volume as against table wines which average about 12%. A new law allows 18% dessert wines and 17% Sherries. Most major wineries are shifting to the lower strengths. The higher alcoholic content is obtained by adding brandy during the fermentation of the wine. The earlier it is added, the sweeter the resulting wine will be.

The appellation of origin and the varietal designation are not nearly as usual with the California aperitif and dessert wines, as with the table wine types. With the exception, in some brands, of the Palomino grape in sherry, of the Tinta varieties in port, of Muscat Frontignan and of a few other minor instances, mention of varietal designation is absent. Most of them are also simply labeled as "California" without further indication of origin. This is a pity for just as the northern coastal counties produce the finest table wines, it is the Great Inland Valley Region that is best suited, on account of its warm to hot climate, for the production of aperitif and dessert wines. It is to be hoped that one day the fact that a Sherry or Port from either the Lodi or Fresno district, for instance, will mean as much to the public as a fine varietal table wine hailing from one of the outstanding northern coastal counties.

A. *CALIFORNIA SHERRY*

The main characteristic of sherry, wherever it is produced, is its more or less pronounced *nutty* flavor, and it is to this end that the grower develops his basic wine. Most suitable for its production in California, as in its native Spain, is the Palomino grape, also known in some wine growing districts of California as the Golden Chasselas and it is from this grape that all the finer California sherries are derived. The fact is then often indicated on the label.

California sherries are produced by two entirely different methods. Most of them are treated by the so-called heating or "baking" method, similar to that used for Madeira wines in the island of that name off the coast of West Africa. California *flor* sherries owe their special character to a process resembling that used in Spain for Spanish sherries of the drier types.

In the heating method the basic wine is fermented to the desired degree of dryness, brandy being added to check the fermentation. It is then heated in oak, redwood, concrete or steel containers for a number of weeks or months up to a year at a temperature of about 120 degrees Fahrenheit. This takes place in heated cellars or by the vats being heated by coils and at times by the warmth of the sun. When the process is completed the wine is gradually cooled and aged for the desired period of time. The oxidation taking place during the heating of the wine gives it the typical character associated with sherry.

In the *flor* process the wines usually undergo primary fermentation by a standard wine yeast to dryness. They are then fortified to ca. 15% alcohol and the growing cells of *Saccharomyces beticus* are placed on the wine's surface. This yeast, covering the wine with a flowerlike crust (hence the term *flor*), lives on the alcohol and other wine constituents and imparts to the wine, by some mysterious alchemy of nature, the characteristic flavor and tang of sherry. The wine, when fully impregnated, is brought up to full alcoholic strength and then blended and aged by the so-called "Solera" system.

This true *flor* process has been largely replaced in recent years by the "submerged *flor*" method developed at the University of California at Davis, in which yeast cells are conditioned to grow aerobically in deep tank cultures with agitation. The process is not unlike that used to produce antibiotics.

California wineries have adopted their own Solera systems which vary considerably, resembling to a greater or lesser degree the method by which sherries are aged and blended in Spain. Basically a Solera consists of an arrangement of communicating barrels or vats lying in superimposed rows, four to five tiers high. At periodic intervals the matured sherry is drawn from the bottom row to be bottled, this row being replenished from the row above and so on to the top range which is filled with new wine. In this manner the young wine mixes and ages with the older in one perpetual blend while the Solera itself was started with aged wine in the first place.

Pale or Cocktail Sherry

The drier sherries, varying from very pale and very dry to amber and dry. Some producers bottle both a Pale Dry *and* a Cocktail Sherry, the former being usually the paler and the drier of the two.

Sherry or Golden Sherry

The medium dry to medium sweet types, golden amber in color. California Sherry, without further indication, falls in this class, as does Amber Sherry.

Sweet Sherry or Cream Sherry

The sweet types, usually of a dark amber color.

Marsala

California *Marsala* is the result of a sherry blend trying to approach the character of the well-known Marsala wines from Sicily, so popular also in cooking. Herb flavored California Marsalas have also been produced.

Madeira

A few firms, following the lead of Paul Masson, now market California Madeira, similar to medium or sweet sherry.

B. *CALIFORNIA PORT*

Port has been made in California at least since the days of the Gold Rush and is one of the most popular of the so-called "dessert wines." It is often used as an aperitif as well as between meals or after dinner. Conforming to the American taste California port is, on the whole, sweeter than the port wines from Portugal. There is also, oddly enough, hardly any California *dry* port produced.

California port is produced from many different grapes, only a few of which are used for the wine in its native Portugal. To this selected group belong the popular Tinta Madeira, which yields an excellent varietal wine, Tinta Cão (sometimes blended with the former to yield Tinta port), Alvarelhão, Souzão and Touriga. Another is the Trousseau which has been identified as the Portuguese Bastardo.

California ports are generally sweet, rich, heavy bodied and fruity but often rather bland and neutral in flavor unless produced from the finer and more flavorful grapes. Young port wine, like young sherry, is apt to be "hot" to the taste buds. Older ports, and those where the better brandy has been used in their production, are naturally smoother and mellower. Some will throw a deposit and should be decanted.

Tinta Madeira

A varietal port wine made from the grape of that name and outstanding in character and flavor and fruitiness.

Tinta Port

Produced from one or more of the grapes bearing a Tinta (meaning red) name, such as Tinta Madeira, Tinta Cão. Another very fine wine.

Vintage Port

Derived from grapes harvested in a particular year. Vintage ports are usually fortified with low proof pot still brandy and bottled after one to two years wood age, so that crust may develop in the bottle. Vintage ports should be decanted.

Port and Ruby Port

Most wines labeled simply as port are ruby red and could equally well have been marketed as Ruby Port. There is often little difference, if any, between the two types when produced by the same grower.

Tawny Port

This can be a port that has been aged for considerable time in the wood, the original ruby red color turning to a russet or tawny shade.

It can also be a port made from grapes like the Trousseau which naturally yields a wine of a tawny hue.

In the cheaper brands there is often little or no difference between the tawny and other red port types, and the tawny color is the result of "baking" similar to sherry.

White Port

Nothing to do with port at all, this sweet wine is very light in color and neutral in flavor with little, if anything, to recommend it. Sometimes a decolorization process is applied to ensure its light color.

C. *CALIFORNIA MUSCATEL* and *MUSCAT*

These are among the sweetest of all wines and are of very ancient origin, being mentioned in literature more than 2000 years ago. The great center of California's muscat cultivation lies in the San Joaquin Valley where the grapes attain their maximum sugar content.

Muscat Frontignan

The finest California varietal muscat, delicate, golden and very sweet with a strong muscat perfume and flavor. The name is derived from the French town of Frontignan well known for its muscat wines. The grape is called Muscat Canelli from its original home of Canelli near Asti in Piedmont, Italy, where it is famed for Italian muscat wines, both still and sparkling.

Malvasia Bianca (White Malvasia)

Made from the muscat flavored grape of the same name this varietal wine, containing 20% alcohol, should not be confused with the white table wine of the same name (see there).

There is also a red Malvasia wine, produced in Southern California.

Aleatico

A soft, fruity, aromatic sweet varietal wine, sometimes called Red Muscatel. Some is produced in Southern California. At one time the grape was used to make a table wine of the same name.

Black Muscat

This is a name given to high quality red muscatels produced from Muscat Hamburg grapes or from a blend of these and Aleatico. It is one of California's foremost wines of the "dessert" type and to be recommended also as an appetizer when used with a slice of lemon.

Muscatel

Generally made from the Muscat of Alexandria grape which does so well in the San Joaquin Valley and in the Escondido district in San Diego County.

The wine varies from light to dark amber and from sweet to very sweet. It has a pronounced muscat aroma and flavor if properly made from Muscat of Alexandria grapes for considerably more than the minimum legal percentage of 51%. It is then actually a varietal although this is rarely indicated on the label.

D. *ANGELICA*

Said to have been named after the city of Los Angeles, this is one of the sweetest of all wines. Since California's early days it has been traditionally associated with the Mission grape from which much of the wine is still made. The excessive sweetness is obtained by arresting fermentation at an early stage so the must retains much of its sugar content. Amber in color, it is smooth and liqueurlike without varietal character.

E. *CALIFORNIA TOKAY*

A hybrid wine of little charm unrelated in any way to the renowned Tokay wines of Hungary.

California Tokay, amber pink in color, is a blend of angelica or other neutral wine, sherry to give a slight nutty taste, and port to lend it color. Occasionally the Flame Tokay grape, which makes such a brilliant display of its foliage in the autumn around Lodi, is used in the wine's production.

F. *CALIFORNIA VERMOUTH*

Vermouth is named after its most typical flavoring ingredient, wormwood, derived from the woody herb of that name, called *Wermuth* in German. A white wine is used as base while much of the flavoring material is imported. The wine is brought to the desired alcoholic strength and either infused and later filtered or an extract is simply added to it. Besides wormwood a host of other flavorings are used, exactly which depending on the producer and the brand.

There are two main kinds of California Vermouth, the sweet and the dry but the very light and very dry type has won separate recognition. No white *sweet* vermouth is produced, which seems a pity.

Dry Vermouth

This type is also known as French Vermouth as the wine originated and became famous in France. California Dry Vermouth is pale golden or light amber in color and averages about 18% alcohol by volume. It is made with a neutral white wine base of relatively high acid content which is fortified and blended and to which about half an ounce of herb mixture or extract is added per gallon of wine to obtain the desired character.

Light Dry Vermouth (Extra Dry, Very Dry, Triple Dry, Dry White)

A very light and very dry vermouth created to satisfy (it is hoped) advocates of the driest and palest of dry martinis.*

Sweet Vermouth

Also known as Italian Vermouth as it originated in that country. It is reddish amber to brown in color, aromatic, quite sweet and contains about 16% alcohol by volume.

White wine, traditionally with some muscat, is used as a base to which one to one and a half ounces of herbs are added per gallon to give the wine its desired character. It is then aged in wooden casks but for only a short period of time to prevent loss of aroma through volatilization.

* Happily the craze for ever drier and ever paler martinis seems on the wane so that the danger of a vermouthless martini looms less large than it did some years ago. How straight or nearly straight gin can taste good to anyone remains a mystery to this writer. Three to four parts of gin to one of dry vermouth seems just about right, depending on the brands used. For the smoothest martinis try mixing them a few hours before, adding a strip of lemon peel and storing them in the freezer.

In response to an earlier edition advocating storage of martinis overnight in the refrigerator, Professor James F. Guymon of the University of California wrote: "I personally disagree with mixing martinis ahead of time. Refrigerator temperature is never as low (i.e. not cold enough) as the alcohol-melting ice mixture which can be less than o degrees C. or 32 degrees F."

VIII

FLAVORED WINES

*S*o-called "flavored wines" have made their appearance on the American market in large numbers in the relatively recent past and warrant special notice.

These wines carry proprietary names and generally have a citrus or herb flavoring. They are usually sweet (10 to 14% sugar content) and generally have the same alcoholic content (20%) as the regular types of aperitif and dessert wines.

A flavored wine may be designated legally as an aperitif wine if it contains herbs in a sufficient degree to be detected by a tasting test. Wines that do not contain herbs or that contain herbs in such minute amounts that they are not detectable in such a test may not legally be designated as aperitifs. Hence the term "flavored wines."

Exactly which flavors and herbs are used depends on the individual wine and its producer. Predominant use is made of natural citric flavors, primarily lemon and lime, and of fruit flavors such as blackberry, cherry, loganberry and raspberry. The use of rose, violet, pure vanilla and herb extractions is also indicated.

These wines are sometimes called "natural flavored wines" as the flavoring used in them is natural and not artificial or chemical.

IX

CALIFORNIA FRUIT WINES

A. *BERRY WINES*

*F*RUIT WINES are produced by fermentation of fruits other than grapes, ameliorized with sugar. Most of them average around 12% alcohol by volume but a few types are also marketed at 20%, the latter being produced by the addition of spirits or of brandy from the same kind of fruit from which the wine was made.

Berry Wines

California has the largest berry production of any state in the union. All berry wines are fruity and sweet, each with the typical character and more or less pronounced flavor of the particular berry from which it is derived.

Blackberry Wines

The blackberry or bramble is a native of temperate regions and is particularly abundant on the Pacific Coast. There are over 600 named varieties of the blackberry of which the boysenberry (see below) is the best known for wine production in California.

Blackberry wine is produced at both 12% and 20% alcohol by volume.

Blackberry Wine of the Boysenberry Variety

Boysenberries constitute by far the greater part of the blackberries grown in the United States. They are black when ripe with a slight blue or purple tinge. The wine they yield has an especially distinctive aroma and flavor. It is produced both at 12% and at 20% alcohol by volume.

Elderberry Wine

This wine is made from the umbrella shaped berry clusters of the American or sweet elder. It is purplish red and has the typical tangy flavor of the fruit. 12% alcohol by volume.

Loganberry Wine

The berry was named after Judge J. H. Logan who raised it from seed in his garden at Santa Cruz, California, in 1881. The wine is brilliant red and has a pronounced fruity flavor. 12% alcohol by volume.

Raspberry Wine

Made from the red raspberry and having the delicate aroma and flavor of that fruit. 12% alcohol by volume.

Red Currant Wine

Produced from the small tangy berries of the red currant shrub from which the popular jelly is also made. The wine is light red, less sweet than other berry wines and contains 12% alcohol by volume.

Strawberry Wine

California's Santa Clara Valley is famed for its strawberries. Much of the strawberry wine is also produced there. It is delicate in flavor and has an alcoholic content of 12% by volume.

B. *FRUIT WINES OTHER THAN BERRY WINES*

Apple Wine

California apple wine is made princpially from Gravenstein apples which are specially well suited for the purpose because of their flavor, high sugar content and juiciness. They are grown mainly in the vicinity of Santa Rosa and Sebastopol in Sonoma County. The wine is usually bottled at 20% alcohol by volume.

Apricot Wine

Although this beverage is not produced in large quantities in California, it, as is cherry wine, is popular with Scandinavian-Americans. The alcohol content usually is about 12% by volume.

Cherry Wine

The best cherry wine is made from the sour or pie type cherry which gives the wine a brilliant red color and a pronounced fruity flavor. 12% alcohol by volume.

Peach Wine

A less familiar fruit wine, containing 12% or 20% alcohol by volume.

Pear Wine also called **Perry**

Occasionally met with and containing 12% alcohol by volume.

Part Two

X

NOTABLE WINERIES BY
REGION AND DISTRICT

*T*HERE ARE two accepted ways of classifying the wine growing districts of California.

The first, as worked out by the viticultural scientists of the University of California, is of primary interest to the growers. The method
is based on the adaptability of the different grape varieties to the
climatic conditions of the various wine growing localities of the
state. These have been grouped, regardless of location, according to
the average degrees of heat above 50° Fahrenheit from April 1 to
October 31, and correspond to what can be termed the cool, moderately cool, intermediate, moderately hot and hot climatic zones.

The type of soil, naturally, also influences the grape as to the character of the wine it will yield. Even so, the vine draws much of its
nourishment from the surrounding atmosphere, the leaves of all
plants nourishing themselves by breathing in the air.

The second system is the geographical one, which makes it possible to progress from region to region and from district to district or
county. This makes it easy to follow the various wine growing districts on a map and is the method utilized by this *Guide.*

The geographical system is also preferable for the purpose of this

Guide, as many wineries obtain grapes, and sometimes wines, from vineyards located in more than one climatic zone, be it from their own vines or from other growers, and either from the same general area or from other districts. Growers in the inland valley often produce table wines from grapes grown in the coastal districts, or blend them with the valley wines, and coastal growers often make aperitif and dessert types from grapes grown in the inland valley areas.

Whether or not a wine has been wholly produced by the grower is indicated on the labeling. The term "produced and bottled" means that a minimum of 75% of the wine has been produced, that is, fermented into wine, by the grower whose name appears on the label. "Made and bottled" means that at least 10% of the wine has actually been produced and that the balance has received some cellar treatment by the grower on the label, although it may not have been produced in his winery. The difference between the two methods of production does not necessarily indicate a graduation in quality among wines, although wineries are naturally the proudest of those wines which they themselves have wholly grown and produced. Wineries which only market the latter are sometimes described as having a chateau operation. Such wines are, or can be designated as "estate bottled."

The more notable wineries of California are presented in the following pages by region and district. In each district they are arranged alphabetically within the locality. Selection has been governed by the quality, both of premium and standard quality wines produced. No prices are indicated, as they will vary according to the part of the country where they are purchased.

A complete listing of all California wineries is published in the "Annual Directory Issue" of the publication *Wines and Vines,** while a practical series of Guide Maps, arranged by county, is available at the Wine Institute.†

* 703 Market Street, San Francisco 94103.
† 717 Market Street, San Francisco 94103.

The California wine producing areas can be grouped geographically in three great regions, as follows:

The cool to moderately cool *northern coastal region,* where all the finest table wines are produced, the top quality champagnes, and some notable aperitif and dessert wines.

The hot inland valley region, the home especially of the aperitif and dessert wines, but producing also table wines and bulk fermented champagnes.

The warm *Southern California region,* where aperitif and dessert wines, champagnes, and table wines of note are produced.

XI

THE NORTHERN COASTAL REGION

*T*HIS REGION, sometimes referred to as that of the northern coastal counties, lies close to the coast north and south of San Francisco and takes in the wine growing districts west of the coastal range of mountains. They are, from north to south:

The *Sonoma-Mendocino, Napa Valley-Solano, Alameda-Contra Costa* and the *Santa Clara-Santa Cruz-San Benito* districts, lying respectively northwest, northeast, southeast and south of the Golden Gate. The city of San Francisco, where a few wineries are located, is treated as a separate district.

A. *SONOMA-MENDOCINO DISTRICT*

This district consists of the two counties which have given it their joint names. Sonoma County yields some premium table wines and champagnes which rate among the finest of the state. It also produces vast quantities of standard quality table wine, mostly red.

Sonoma, with nearly thirty bonded wineries and wine cellars, ranks third behind Napa and Santa Clara among all California counties in number of winemaking plants. Its wines can conveniently be grouped according to the three valleys where they are produced: the Sonoma, Santa Rosa and Russian River valleys.

Sonoma County—Sonoma Valley

The appellation Sonoma Valley is restricted in the *Guide* to denote the valley proper. The name has often been loosely applied to a larger area, taking in the neighboring Santa Rosa Valley, but the latter is actually part of the Russian River basin and is therefore treated separately. Sonoma Valley is some eleven miles long and is named after Sonoma Creek, which empties in San Pablo Bay to the south.

Sonoma Valley is familiar to many as the Valley of the Moon, made famous in literature by Jack London, who wrote and died there, not far from the ruins of the once famous Kohler winery, destroyed by the great earthquake of 1906.

The Valley of the Moon, or of the Moons, as the Indians used to call it, does its name full justice, for, separated from the Napa Valley to the east by the Mayacamas Range, the moon, to those down below, seems to rise, not once, but many times among the succeeding mountain peaks.

Buena Vista Winery Inc., Sonoma

It seems only suitable to begin the presentation of the wineries of California with Buena Vista, once the home of Haraszthy, the "father of modern California viticulture."

Agoston Haraszthy, a man of temperament and of many talents, came from a noble Hungarian family. Because of wanderlust or because he aided in plotting Magyar independence, he left his Hungarian domain and sailed for America. He first settled in Wisconsin, where he founded the town of Haraszthy, which was to become Sauk City. Known as the "Count," he later shed this title for the more democratic one of "Colonel."

In 1849 he came West, to San Diego, which he helped to develop and where he was elected the town's first sheriff. He later represented that county as state assemblyman and moved north to Sacramento. San Francisco, thriving with the Gold Rush, next attracted the colonel's energetic spirit and he became the official melter and refiner of the U.S. Mint. He landed in difficulties, accused of exceeding his legal limit of gold wastage, but was absolved by the court and his name completely cleared.

Haraszthy had been interested in viticulture ever since his early Hungarian days. In California he had planted vineyards near San Diego and in San Francisco near Mission Dolores as well as at Crystal Springs, in what is now San Mateo. He realized, from the example of Jean Louis Vignes at Los Angeles, that the better California wines were produced from European grape varieties and he himself had already imported many such vines, including, as had been widely accepted, the one he named and became known as Zinfandel.

Haraszthy finally chose Sonoma as the ideal place to realize his ambition of establishing the finest vineyards in California. He became a neighbor of the pioneer grower General Vallejo, who produced a wine of great repute, Lachryma Montis, named after his estate. The two families became friendly rivals in wine making, and became much closer than friends when the double wedding took place at the Mission San Francisco de Solano in Sonoma in 1863, uniting Natalia and Jovita, daughters of General Vallejo, to Attila and Arpad Haraszthy, sons of the colonel.

Haraszthy had named his country place Buena Vista because of the sweeping view of the Sonoma Valley and San Francisco Bay and here he constructed an imposing Pompeian mansion. Hundreds of acres of vines were planted and a series of tunnels dug deep in the hillside for cellar accommodation. Skilled viticulturists came to work at Buena Vista, among them Charles Krug, who was himself to become one of California's leading wine growers.

It was a Buena Vista that Haraszthy wrote his classic "Report on Grapes and Wines of California." He advised all growers to test as many varieties as possible, to cultivate those which throve the best and produced the finest wines. He was certain that California could yield "as noble a wine as any country on the face of the globe."

In 1861 Haraszthy was appointed by Governor John G. Downey to report on wine growing in Europe. From a viticultural point of view the trip was a great success. He visited all the important European wine growing districts and collected some 100,000 cuttings from 300 grape varieties, all of which he planted on his return. Financially the journey proved a source of discord. The California Legislature refused to pay the expenses incurred, but the colonel could find consolation in being made president of the California Agricultural Society. Haraszthy had reached the summit of his prestige. The fame of Buena Vista wines had spread far; offices of the company were operating in San Francisco, in Chicago, New York, Philadelphia and London. In October 1864 Colonel and Mrs. Haraszthy were hosts at a Vintage Ball and Masquerade, the social event of the time.

Then financial and other troubles succeeded each other rapidly. Phylloxera struck, Haraszthy suffered losses on the Stock Exchange, taxes on spirits wiped out his profit on brandy, a fire raged at Buena Vista, ruining much of the wine, credit was cut off from the bank, and financial assistance from other sources proved unavailable.

So the "father of California's modern wine industry" left Buena Vista, Sonoma, and California for good. He went to Nicaragua, where he obtained a government contract for the distillation of spirits from sugar and there he started a new domain. But one day, in July 1869, he vanished. It is believed that he tried to cross an alligator infested stream by means of an overhanging branch which broke off by his weight and plunged him to his doom. The life of a great American pioneer had come to a tragic end.

In California Attila and Arpad Haraszthy continued the family wine making tradition. Arpad became famous for his "Eclipse" Champagne, while Attila stayed on at Buena Vista to fight the phylloxera, which was not conquered till the turn of the century. The estate suffered a further great blow when the 1906 earthquake brought down in ruins much of the winery and caved in the storage tunnels, burying, so it is believed, much champagne beneath the debris. Buena Vista entered a dormant period in wine making which lasted till 1943.

In that year Frank H. Bartholomew, now chairman of the board of United Press International (U.P.I.), acquired a large acreage of the former Buena Vista vineyards and revived the society, restoring also the two stone wineries from Harazsthy's days.

In 1968, a $2 million corporation was formed to construct a third winery building. The winery itself was sold to Young's Markets of Los Angeles and Bartholomew, who remains as Buena Vista's president, retained the vineyards and ranch. Vernon O. Underwood of Los Angeles, president of Young's, joined the company as chairman of the board. Philip C. Gaspar is general manager.

The following premium wines are available under the *Buena Vista* label:

Table wines:
> RED: Cabernet Sauvignon (Estate Bottled), Pinot Noir, Zinfandel (from the vineyards where the wine grew to fame), Burgundy;
> WHITE: Pinot Chardonnay (Estate Bottled), White Riesling Johannisberger (Estate Bottled), Gewurztraminer (Estate Bottled, Vintage), Sylvaner (Estate Bottled, Vintage), Sonoma Sauterne (Vintage), Green Hungarian (a *Buena Vista* specialty), Chablis, Vine Brook (from *Sylvaner* grapes, Vintage), Grey Riesling (Estate Bottled);
> ROSÉ: Rose Brook (from Cabernet Sauvignon grapes, Estate Bottled) and Grenache Rosé;

Champagne (Bottle fermented): Pinot Chardonnay Champagne (Brut, Estate grown);

Sparkling: Burgundy, Cabernet Sauvignon Rose;

Aperitif and Dessert Wines: Ultra Dry Sherry, Golden Sherry and Cardinal Port (all finished in small oak casks).

Hanzell Vineyards, Sonoma

The reason for the existence of the beautiful Hanzell Vineyards high in the hills behind Sonoma overlooking the romantic Valley of the Moon is simple but inspiring.

After returning home from Italy where he had served as Chief of the Marshall Plan from 1948 to 1950 the well known businessman, financier and diplomat J. D. Zellerbach and Mrs. Zellerbach bought a country place in the Sonoma Valley. Highly appreciative of fine wines the thought came naturally to establish vineyards on the hillsides sloping down from the house. A perfectionist and partial to the great burgundies of France, Mr. Zellerbach had his vineyards of some 16 acres planted exclusively to Pinot noir and Chardonnay, responsible for the glories of his favorite Romanée Conti and Montrachet. From that developed the idea of building a model winery and making his own wine, the finest California could produce. It was to be an operation in the grand manner and great traditions. Experts, including sages of the University of California, were consulted in the layout of the vineyards and in equipping the winery, inspired by Burgundy's Clos de Vougeot. No effort was spared in securing the best of everything. Winery equipment was specially designed at great expense, glass lined stainless steel tanks of the most modern type were installed, small Limousin oak cooperage was imported from Nuits St. Georges in Burgundy and an up to date and efficient laboratory was provided. The winery was named Hanzell Vineyards, a contraction of Hana, as Mrs. Zellerbach is called, and of the family name.

When Ambassador Zellerbach died just before the 1963 harvest, many connoisseurs wondered out loud what would happen to his "great experiment." They were relieved when Hanzell wines, made with exactly the same care and devotion as before, returned to the market under the aegis of the late Douglas N. Day, a retired supermarket chain executive who purchased the Zellerbach Sonoma estate in 1965. His first crush took place that fall, and the wines, still Pinot Noir and Chardonnay exclusively, were bottled in 1967. Mr. Day died in 1970, and was replaced by his widow.

The new owners altered little at Hanzell. Bradford Webb, the winery's original chemist and *maître de chai,* was retained as chief consultant. The winemaker now is Kim Giles. New Limousin oak barrels from France replaced those casks removed from the winery when the previous vintages were sold by the Zellerbach estate.

To the Days, operating the winery is not a business, "it's more like raising a child."

"The objective that motivated the development of Hanzell continues to prevail today," Mr. Day said. "Many knowledgeable enophiles consider that the two wines of Hanzell are the two finest of their types produced in California. Certainly the current demand for the wines is sufficient tribute. We have been forced to accept orders on a reservation basis only."

Since her husband's death, Mrs. Day has added another storage room for Pinot Noir and has cleared four more acres to plant Chardonnay vines grafted from the same stocks in the original vineyards. Even so, she said, "the demand for our Chardonnay is far greater than we can supply."

Sebastiani Vineyards, Sonoma

This winery, one of the largest producers in Sonoma County and the oldest wine enterprise in the Sonoma Valley operated continuously by one family, was founded in 1904 by Samuele Sebastiani who immigrated from Italy at an early age. From a small beginning—the 501 gallon tank he purchased from the old Bullotti Winery—he gradually built up his enterprise through hard work, a strong determination to succeed and a deep faith in spiritual assistance.

During the 40 years that Samuele Sebastiani was a prominent figure in the Sonoma wine industry his operation grew to be Northern California's largest individually owned winery with a cooperage of one and three quarters million gallons. He shared his success with many about him, building homes for his workers and donating a parochial school. For the people of Sonoma he built streets for the town, an apartment house, a theatre, an auto court, recreational facilities and completed many other projects.

When Samuele Sebastiani retired his son August took over, putting much energy into wine making, distillation processes and improvements in general. His father, however, never failed to visit the winery until his death in 1944.

Some vineyards are owned in the Sonoma Valley but most of the wines are produced from grapes purchased year after year from the same growers. The winery's operation was mostly on a bulk wine basis supplying other wineries and bottlers throughout the nation when August Sebastiani decided in 1954 to begin bottling his own wines. Much money went into research while the know-how and experience were already present. To get the full flavor of the Sebastiani enterprise let us quote August Sebastiani owner and general manager:

"We inherit that peculiarly favorable grape soil of Sonoma, a bountiful sky of rain and sunshine, and a people willing to work and to take great pride in their product. We are proud of what we produce."

There is no doubt that August Sebastiani is a man who inherits the love of wine making from his father and who possesses the industrial skill of an organizer with modern ideas based on old but dynamic and proved methods. A charming host and a dedicated person he lives with his closely knit family on a hilltop right in Sonoma not far from his beloved winery. Many medals in the winery's sampling room testify to the family ability in wine making.

Sebastiani Vineyards produces tables wines, aperitif and dessert wines, including vermouths. August Sebastiani is particularly proud of his Tuscan wine making methods. The rewards are obvious in his Barbera, a hearty, ruby red varietal. He and his able and energetic son, Sam, also have a right to be pleased with the public response to their Green Hungarian, Gamay Beaujolais and Zinfandel.

In the summer of 1971 the Sebastianis completed a sun-heated aging area for Solera Sherries and Ports.

ZD Wines, Sonoma

The name of this new operation in the tiny hamlet of Vineburg hard by Sonoma comes from the last initials of the partners who own it, Gino Zepponi and Norman deLeuze. Aerospace and optics engineers respectively, they established the winery in 1969 as a hobby and retirement plan. Their first wines, Pinot Noir and White Riesling, were produced that year, and a Gewurztraminer was added in 1970.

All ZD wines are and will be 100 per cent varietals, the partners said, and all are aged in 50-gallon oak casks in their small but efficient air-conditioned winery. Although they started without their own vineyard, they planned to crush 20 tons in 1971 from carefully-tended farms nearby. Zepponi also has planted a small Chardonnay vineyard which is expected to be in full production by 1973.

Visits to the winery must be arranged by mail, the same method by which most ZD wines are sold.

SONOMA COUNTY—SANTA ROSA VALLEY

The Santa Rosa Creek, after which the valley is named, empties its waters eventually in the Russian River. The city of Santa Rosa is where the Luther Burbank home is to be found. The famed botanist and horticulturist, who was also greatly interested in viticulture, lies buried beneath the cedar of Lebanon in the city park.

Martini & Prati Wines, Inc., Santa Rosa

Some eight miles northwest of Santa Rosa, near Forestville, lies the extensive Martini and Prati Winery, operated by Elmo Martini* and Edward Prati.

The Martini family have been in the wine business in Santa Rosa since the eighteen seventies. Raphaele Martini bought the present winery and vineyards shortly after the turn of the century, the enterprise being expanded at various times and later operated by his sons. In 1943 the property was purchased by the Hiram Walker interests, owners of W. A. Taylor and Company, but in 1950 the winery and vineyards reverted back to Elmo Martini, in partnership with Enrico Prati of Italian Swiss Colony fame and with the latter's son Edward. Enrico Prati passed away in 1952 and Elmo Martini is now president

* Not to be confused with Louis Martini of St. Helena, Napa County.

of the company, while Edward Prati, who also owns vineyards of his own, is secretary-treasurer.

The winery is the second largest in Sonoma County. The featured brands are *Martini & Prati* and *Fountaingrove,* the latter label having been purchased from the owner of Fountaingrove Ranch, once a famed winery.

Sonoma County—Russian River Valley

The Russian River finds its source in Mendocino County and flows south into Sonoma, turning west past Healdsburg to empty in the Pacific Ocean some ten miles beyond Guerneville.

The lower Russian River Valley, around Guerneville, forms a small, separate wine growing area, where some of the finest California champagne is produced. The inland or upper section of the valley takes in the area around Healdsburg northwards to Cloverdale and on into Mendocino County.

F. Korbel & Brothers, Inc., Guerneville

The great, castle-like Korbel winery, standing among vineyards and huge tree stumps, is situated on the bank of the Russian River a few miles east of Guerneville, just beyond Rio Nido. It is the home of champagnes that rate among the finest of California and are known throughout the nation and beyond.

It was founded by the Korbels, a story of enterprise dating back to the days of the pioneers.

The Korbel brothers, Francis, Anton and Joseph, were born in the little town of Behine in Bohemia, now part of Czechoslovakia. They emigrated to the United States and came to San Francisco in the early eighteen sixties. Ironworkers and machinists by trade they soon found employment in machine shops. Francis, the eldest, built a cigar box factory, aided by his brothers, and such was the beginning of a family enterprise that led by stages to lithography, lumber, the building of a sawmill on the Russian River and finally to the production of wine and champagne.

When all the virgin timber had been cut—the vast stumps of which remain an impressive sight today—the Korbels sought the advice of the University of California on what to raise on the newly cleared land. After a dairy venture that proved unsuccessful vines were planted with the purpose of selling the grapes to Sonoma wineries. When the first crop was harvested grape prices proved to be so low that the Korbels decided to crush the grapes themselves and so they landed in the wine business.

The original winery still stands and in 1886 the first section of the present winery was constructed from lumber and brick made on the property. Table wines were produced at first but in the nineties it was decided to make champagne as well and the latter became the sole business of Korbel Brothers after the second World War.

In early 1954 the Korbel family, headed by Anton and Leo Korbel, sold the corporation to the Heck brothers, another dynasty of wine makers. Adolf L. Heck is president of the company and the champagne producer, Paul R. is executive vice president, taking care of the 2,200 acre ranch and of the initial wine production while Ben A. Heck is vice president in charge of sales.

The grandfather of the Heck brothers started the family wine business by owning and operating a small winery in Alsace-Lorraine, at that time part of Germany. His son, Adolf Heck, the father of the Heck brothers, knew about wine making from an early age, and came to this country shortly after the turn of the century, going into the wine business in Chicago. In 1933, with the advent of Repeal, the family moved to St. Louis where Adolf Heck senior took over the operation of the American Wine Company, producers at that time of Cook's Imperial Champagne. He remained president and general manager until his death in 1946. The American Wine Company having been acquired by the Schenley interests, the Heck brothers went with National Distillers, remaining in the wine business at Italian Swiss Colony. In 1954 the opportunity arose to buy the Korbel winery, something the Heck brothers had been waiting for. And so the name of Heck became identified with that of Korbel in the field of premium wine making.

Quality is the Heck brothers philosophy. They do not believe in making the public drink what they think it should have but rather in giving the public what it wants and making it as well as possible. The most important varietal grapes raised at the ranch for the production of sparkling wines are Pinot noir, Pinot blanc, Chardonnay, French Colombard and Sauvignon blanc. Some White Riesling and Sylvaner are also grown.

Under the ownership of the Heck brothers bottle fermented Champagnes continue to be featured, made by the original French Champagne process. They are marketed under the *Korbel* brand, as follows:

Korbel Natura (very dry, made especially for gourmets), Korbel Brut (dry), Korbel Extra Dry (medium dry), Korbel Sec (medium dry), Korbel Rouge (red champagne or sparkling burgundy, on the dry side) and Korbel Rosé (a pink champagne marketed in a transparent bottle, delicately sweet).

The Heck brothers added a light brandy to their line, and within 10 years it became one of the largest-selling in California. Later, they entered the aperitif and dessert wine field, and now offer four in addition to a complete line of table wines. All are sold under the *Korbel* label, including Chablis, Sauterne, Grey Riesling, Rosé, Burgundy, Cabernet, Pinot Noir, Cocktail Sherry, Medium Sherry, Cream Sherry and Port.

In 1954 the Heck brothers purchased the nearby Santa Nella winery and have since remodeled to provide facilities for all of Korbel's crushing, fermenting and intermediate storage. A new bottling plant for table wines and a case goods warehouse have been added adjacent to the main winery building.

Windsor Vineyards (Tiburon Vintners), Windsor

This company was founded in 1960 by Rodney D. Strong, who remains its board chairman. In 1963 he took over a 68-year-old winery at Windsor eight miles north of Santa Rosa, and at the time of this writing, the corporation he established with Peter Friedman, now president, owns or controls eight new or rehabilitated Sonoma

County vineyards totaling 1,400 acres. The vineyard manager is Richard McDowell and the chemist is Richard Arrowhead.

In 1971 the company dedicated a new $1.5 million winery complex, one of the most modern in the state. The 30,000-square-foot structure took a year to build, and is a far cry from the days when Strong bought bulk wines from other makers, bottled and labelled them under his own name.

Tiburon Vintners markets its products direct from the winery to the consumer only, and it is one of the few wineries in the world which specializes in preparing each case with personally inscribed labels to honor any individual or commemorate any occasion. Tasting rooms are maintained at the main office in Tiburon on the north shore of San Francisco Bay and at the winery in Windsor.

In addition to Sherry and Port, most table wines are available under the *Windsor Vineyards* label.

L. Foppiano Wine Company, Healdsburg

The winery dates back to the early eighteen eighties and was known as the Smith winery when the late Louis Foppiano, the father and namesake of the present owner, purchased it in 1898. The company is strictly a family concern.

Louis Foppiano was born right on the property, in the building which now houses the company's offices. Raised in the business since his earliest days, he has built it into a prosperous concern, with vineyards over 200 acres.

Table wines are the specialty, notable among them Zinfandel and Petite Sirah.

J. Pedroncelli Winery, Geyserville

One of the most interesting wineries in Sonoma County is that of the Pedroncelli family, which acquired the vineyards in 1927. John G. Pedroncelli, who restored the original 1904 winery to commercial production after the evil days of Prohibition, has been succeeded by his two sons, co-owners John A. Pedroncelli, general manager, and James Pedroncelli, who is in charge of sales.

Although the winery has been expanded several times, the original wood and concrete building still is in use. Two new concrete block buildings have been added for the aging of wine in small oak casks and bottles. The vineyards are being replanted extensively with emphasis on the classic varietals—Pinot noir, Cabernet Sauvignon, White Riesling, Chardonnay, and Gewurztraminer—and only grapes from the family's and neighboring properties are crushed, giving Pedroncelli wines a definite regional character. All varietals are vintage dated.

Table wines available under the *J. Pedroncelli* label include:

RED: Burgundy, Cabernet Sauvignon, Sonoma Red, Pinot Noir, Zinfandel;

WHITE: Chablis, Johannisberg Riesling, Sonoma White, Chardonnay, Chenin Blanc, Gewurztraminer;

ROSÉ: Sonoma Rosé and Zinfandel Rosé.

Italian Swiss Colony, Asti

The origin of Italian Swiss Colony is in great part the story of Andrea Sbarboro, who came to San Francisco from Italy in the early eighteen fifties as a youngster to work in his brother's grocery store. Twenty years later, by working hard and saving, he bought his own store and turned builder and financier.

In 1881 he founded the Italian Swiss Agricultural Colony with the purpose of aiding Italian and Swiss immigrants to settle in their new land. Many of these were vineyardists by trade and a 1500 acre tract was chosen in Sonoma County, suitable for the planting of vines. The land was named Asti after the town of that name in Piedmont, Italy. Each immigrant was provided with room, board, and wages, in return for which a contribution was expected toward building up an equity in the land and eventually becoming an independent farmer. The immigrants objected to the last condition; they were willing to work, but not to take a chance. Sbarboro decided to operate Asti privately. He set the immigrants to work, planting vines with the idea of growing and selling grapes. The price of the latter soon dropped below the cost of production. It was then decided to press the grapes into wine. The first crush was a disaster owing to carelessness in handling; the wine turned to vinegar.

Asti, so far, had proved a failure, but Sbarboro did not give up. He put Pietro Rossi, a San Francisco druggist who had studied wine making in Italy, in charge of the winery. This was in 1888. The first wines Rossi produced were of good quality but the market price offered for them was unprofitable. The Colony then decided to market its wines direct and set up agencies throughout the country and abroad. Italian Swiss Colony finally came into its own. The fame of its wines soon spread and many medals were received in the United States and Europe and even in the original Asti, in Piedmont.

Sbarboro built a sumptuous mansion at Asti and, being a great practical joker, equipped the gardens with a sprinkler system, copied after the one at Hellbrun in Salzburg. The purpose was not so much to sprinkle his plants, but his guests. The grounds of the estate became a maze of booby traps for the unsuspecting.

With the death of Pietro Rossi, thrown from his horse in 1911, one of the great figures of the Colony passed away. Management of the winery was taken over by his twin sons, Edmund and Robert Rossi, who had been taught the art of wine making by their father. Andrea Sbarboro, who among his other duties headed the Italian-American Bank in San Francisco, remained in charge of the Colony's promotion.

Prohibition was the last enemy to strike at Italian Swiss Colony. Sbarboro proclaimed endlessly that Prohibition was not the road to temperance and appeared before Congress in Washington to protest against this threat to man's liberty of action. But he realized that he was fighting a losing battle. He retired from the wine business and in 1923 he died, partly out of disgust, it is said, that his beloved Asti was bottling grape juice. It was, however, by selling grapes and grape juice that Asti was kept going during Prohibition. When Repeal came, the Rossi twins lost no time in reviving the Colony's wine industry and within a few years Italian Swiss had once again become one of the country's leading wineries.

The "experiment that nearly failed" was finally crowned with solid success. During the second World War Italian Swiss Colony was sold to National Distillers Products Corporation who owned it until April 1953 when it was purchased for a record figure by the Petri family, already well established in the wine industry. The next year the Petris also acquired from National Distillers the popular *Lejon* and *Hartley* Brandy labels and several months later the *Lejon* Vermouth brands. Under the Petri direction *Italian Swiss Colony* and its allied brands continued to grow and expand.

Today the *Italian Swiss Colony* labels are owned by United Vintners Inc., a subsidiary of Heublein Inc. United is said to account for over 25% of the U.S. wine industry volume.

Italian Swiss Colony largely produces and markets medium priced wines of good quality but also sells a limited supply of premium wines under the *Private Stock* label, including aperitif and dessert wines as well as table wines. Generic wines of high quality are also sold by Italian Swiss Colony under the *Tipo* brand. The *Tipo* red and white Chianti are familiar to many, in their straw-covered, flask-shaped bottles, as is the Grenache Rosé.

The usual table and aperitif and dessert wines are marketed under the *Gold Medal Reserve* and *Private Stock* labels, the latter being slightly higher in price and also used for the (bulk fermented) Champagne, Pink Champagne and Sparkling Burgundy. In addition there are specialties such as "Cappella," a Vino Rosso type, and *Italian Swiss Colony* Grenache Vin Rosé, a popular rosé on the sweet side.

The well known *Lejon** Vermouths, both dry and sweet, are now produced by Italian Swiss Colony, as are the *G. & D.*† Vermouths sold in the East. These two brands, it is claimed, dominate the ver-

---

* Named after Lee Jones, a famed figure in the wine industry.
† From Gambarelli & Davitto.

mouth market in the United States. *Lejon* Dry Vermouth, as the author knows by experience, certainly makes an excellent dry martini.

Italian Swiss Colony did much for what has become a popular pastime for the public, the touring of a winery. It is said that over 300,000 people a year now visit the Italian Swiss Colony's comfortable and attractive tasting room at Asti and tour the winery buildings. Near the ivy-covered winery is the original El Carmelo Chapel built by vineyard workers in the shape of a huge wine keg. Next door, a new Roman Catholic church has been built on property donated by I.S.C.

MENDOCINO COUNTY

Fetzer Vineyards, Redwood Valley

Bernard A. Fetzer and his family founded this small, 100-acre operation in 1968, in the seemingly inhospitable semi-wilderness north of Ukiah. Within two years Fetzer wines had earned a solid reputation among connoisseurs. In the words of the owners:

"In this far-north region the vine must put forth maximum effort to survive. The result is wine of much character and finesse. The Fetzer estate is a two-mile long strip of land, canyoned into the slopes of the Pacific Coast Range. The vineyards cover the gravelly benches above Seward and Forsythe Creeks—part of the headwaters of the Russian River. The wines, all vintage and mostly estate bottled, are produced, cellared and bottled at the winery. All red wines are aged in oak casks brought from France."

Although the well-equipped new winery has storage for 50,000 gallons and a bottling capacity of nearly 5,000 cases a week, only 6,000 cases of premium wine are produced annually, with emphasis on estate-bottled Cabernet Sauvignon.

There is no public tasting room, but it is possible to arrange visits by writing to the winery.

Parducci Wine Cellars, Ukiah

This winery is located north of Ukiah and is owned and operated by three generations of the Parducci family. More than half a century of winemaking experience has gone into the growing success of this enterprise.

While the Parduccis originated in Lucca, Italy, Adolph B. Parducci was born in Santa Clara County. As a youngster, however, he went back to the land of his forefathers where he worked in the vineyards, returning to this country at the age of seventeen. In 1918 he founded the Parducci Wine Cellars near Cloverdale in Sonoma County but later, wishing for more space, he moved northwards to Mendocino County finding the suitable location he had been seeking near Ukiah. Here he established his vineyards and in 1931 began construction of the present Parducci Wine Cellars. The winery, surrounded by vineyards, is located in a charming little valley just off the Redwood Highway.

Adolph B. Parducci now is retired and has been succeeded by his sons, John and George, the former being president and winemaker and the latter secretary-treasurer. The third and fourth generations of the family are active in the business.

The usual generic table wines are produced but in recent years the accent has been increasingly placed on the dry varietals. These include Cabernet, Gamay Beaujolais, Pinot Noir and Zinfandel in the reds and Chardonnay, French Colombard, Chenin Blanc, Flora, Semillon and Sylvaner in the whites. Bottle fermented sparkling wines are also featured, including Champagne, both *Brut* and *Extra Dry*, Pink or Rosé Champagne and the inevitable Sparkling Burgundy. Aperitif and dessert wines, including dry and sweet vermouth, are available for the retail trade.

The winery has begun planting its own grapes, and the first production from these was in 1967.

Parducci is the brand used for all wines of premium quality.

B. *NAPA VALLEY—SOLANO. DISTRICT*

This famous district is formed by the two counties bearing those names, with Napa yielding some of the finest of all California table wines.

From a viticultural point of view Napa County and Napa Valley are interchangeable terms, for it is from the valley and its bordering hillsides that the county's famed wines originate. Only the Mayacamas Mountains separate Napa Valley from that of Sonoma, which it parallels. Napa possesses its own romantic name, for in the Indian language it is said to mean "plenty." Napa is indeed the "Valley of Plenty," one of abundant beauty and fertility. Even in ancient times wild grapes are said to have grown here in profusion.

The Napa River which flows through the valley empties, like its Sonoma neighbor, into the waters of San Pablo Bay, connecting with that of San Francisco. Dominating the valley to the north thrones Mt. St. Helena, allegedly christened after that saint by the Princess Helena Gagarin, wife of the one-time Russian Governor of Siberia and of the Russian Northern Pacific Colonies and daughter of the Czar of all the Russias.

Napa County—Upper Napa Valley

Schramsberg Vineyards, Calistoga

This is the successor to the vineyards and winery of Jacob Schram, made famous in literature by Robert Louis Stevenson.

Jacob Schram (or Schramm, as he first spelled it) was a German barber from Johannisberg on the Rhine who did very well in his trade. In 1862 he bought the Mt. Diamond property on the steep hillsides just south of Calistoga, built himself a winery and a mansion, and had a number of cellars dug deep in the mountain. His Schramsberg wines became celebrated, not only in California but in far-off places and are said to have been served at the Carlton Club in London.

The Robert Louis Stevensons, while honeymooning on nearby Mt. St. Helena, visited the Schrams and Stevenson related his impressions in the chapter entitled "Napa Wine" of his *Silverado Squatters*. Fanny Stevenson was entertained by the opulent Mrs. Schram on the veranda of the big house, decorated with a wondrous collection of stuffed birds, while Stevenson and his host tasted one wine after the other in the hillside cellars. He tasted them all, Red Schramsberger and White, Burgundy Schramsberger and Schramsberger Hock. There were varietal wines also and Stevenson dwells on the bouquet of Schramsberger Golden Chasselas. The charm of these wines must have been as great as that of their names, which roll so savorously over the tongue.

After Jacob Schram's death the property was inherited by his son Herman. Prohibition rendered Schramsberg useless for wine making and it was sold to a firm of investment speculators. In 1921 it was acquired by Captain Raymond C. Naylor, who used it as a summer home, and in 1940 Schramsberg was purchased by John Gargano, who had started his California Champagne Company in the early thirties. Gargano had great plans for Schramsberg, but was not able to carry them out because of illness, and he passed away in the beginning of 1952. In 1951 the Schramsberg property was purchased by Douglas Pringle who revived the *Schramsberg* label.

In 1957, the winery was designated by the State of California as a Historical Landmark.

The present history of the winery began in 1965 when Jack L. Davies, an enophile with experience, ambition and dedication, purchased Schramsberg and began its full restoration. Since he wished to produce only bottle-fermented sparkling wines of premium quality, he replanted the vineyards above the winery to Chardonnay and Pinot noir, the principal varieties of France's Champagne District.

The Champagne making itself is carried out in the classical method, with wines aged on the yeast up to three years, depending on variety, before rebottling. The tunnels maintain an even 58-degree temperature throughout the year and provide an excellent environment for bottle-aging. Scramsberg Champagnes normally are vintage-dated and are finished to a very dry edge, bearing no indication of degree of sweetness on the labels.

The wines available under the *Schramsberg* name are as follows:

Blanc de Blancs—a medium-bodied cuvée of Chardonnay and Pinot blanc (offered in regular, reserve and nature grades);

Cuvée de Gamay—a light, tart, pink sparkling wine of the Napa Gamay, and Pinot noir;

Blanc de Noir—a rare wine (white Champagne of the red Pinot noir grape with some Chardonnay), fuller-bodied than the Blanc de Blancs, with the distinctive aroma of Pinot noir.

Sterling Vineyards, Calistoga

In late 1971 construction was started on what was to become one of the most modern and imposing wineries in the upper Napa Valley, a 35,000 square-foot crushing, storage and bottling facility on a hillside overlooking the 400 acres of Sterling Vineyards.

According to Peter L. Newton, president, and Michael Stone, vice president of the owning corporation, the winery eventually would process about 250,000 gallons per year, all from prime varietals and all vintage-dated.

Sterling Vineyards began with a small temporary crushing operation in 1969. None of the wines were on the market at the time of this writing, but international wine authority Robert Lawrence Balzer wrote during the 1970 harvest season, "I've tasted their Merlot '69 from the wood . . . and this 'blending varietal' by itself had rare charms." When it is released for sale it will be the only estate-bottled Merlot, a variety normally used for blending in Bordeaux, in California.

Under the direction of vineyard manager W. Sloan Upton, superintendent Paul Landeros and winemaker R. W. Forman, the vineyards were laid out and pruned to allow mechanical harvesting.

Beringer/Los Hermanos Vineyards, St. Helena

This famous winery, known also as the Los Hermanos Vineyards, was continuously operated as a family concern since its founding in 1876 by the brothers Frederick and Jacob L. Beringer.

Jacob Beringer had learned the art of winemaking in his native Rheingau in Germany as well as in France and when he came to this country his one ambition was to establish a winery and vineyards of his own, such as he had known in Europe. He found the ideal location for his purpose while on a visit to St. Helena and he persuaded his brother Frederick who was already settled in New York in business to come out to California and join him in his project. The result was the founding of the Beringer Brothers' vineyards and winery and of a great name in the California wine industry.

The "Los Hermanos" name was aptly bestowed on the firm by a close friend of the Beringer brothers, Señor Tiburcio Parrott, a Spanish gentleman of the old school who lived in a beautiful villa in St. Helena and was a well known patron of the arts.

A special feature of the winery is the maze of tunnels cut into the limestone hill behind it. There are a thousand feet of this tunneling, originally cut out by Chinese coolies with picks. The tunnels provide an ideal storage space at a steady air conditioned temperature for the aging of wines in fine old casks of oak.

Beringer Bros. was incorporated in 1914 with the descendants of Jacob and Frederick Beringer as members. They sold out in 1971 to the Nestle Co., which installed H. Peter Jurgens, former head of Almaden, as president.

Los Hermanos carries on as of old, but adapting itself to the changing times. While the Beringer policy is to market well aged wines blended so their character and quality remain continuous over the years plans are to concentrate more on the production of varietal table wines. Some 500 acres of new vineyards have been added to 800 already in production.

The featured brand is *Beringer* "Private Stock." Table wines include the regular generic types of which the Sauternes and the Burgundy are the most popular. Varietals include Cabernet Sauvignon, Grignolino, Pinot Noir and Zinfandel in the reds and Johannisberg Riesling, Grey Riesling, Chenin Blanc, Sauvigon Blanc and Chardonnay in the whites. Cabernet and Riesling are also produced.

The usual types of aperitif and dessert wines are marketed, a specialty being Malvasia Bianca, a wine not often met with at 20% alcohol by volume.

Other products featured are Brut Champagne, Pink Champagne and Sparkling Burgundy, not to forget the well known Beringer Brandy.

Chappellet Vineyard, St. Helena

What at least one expert has described as "the best-looking winery built in this century" was completed and bonded just in time for the 1969 harvest by Donn Chappellet, a "dropout" who turned his back on his giant food vending machine empire in Southern California in 1967 and moved his large family to a 100-acre vineyard 1,500 feet up Pritchard Hill above the Napa Valley.

The dun-colored concrete and steel building is laid out in the form of a triangle, the winery's symbol. Chappellet and his vineyardist-winemaker, French-trained Philip Togni, have planted and will bottle only four varieties—Chenin Blanc, Johannisberg Riesling, Chardonnay and Cabernet Sauvignon. The first wine released for sale, the 1968 Chenin Blanc, was made and cellared for Chappellet by friends.

The 45,000-gallon-per-year capacity winery is expected to be in full production by 1975. In the meantime those who find the earlier Chappellet Vineyard wines can count themselves fortunate.

The Christian Brothers' Champagne Cellars, St. Helena

(See The Christian Brothers, Napa)

Freemark Abbey Winery, St. Helena

This is both one of the oldest and one of the newest wineries in the Napa Valley—a highway landmark two miles north of St. Helena built in 1895 by Antonio Forni, out of business by the 1950's, and then recently restored to its original purpose by a partnership of seven vineyard owners and businessmen.

Freemark Abbey is well known to tourists as the location of the Hurd Candle Shop, a gourmet shop and restaurant. The winery is located in the lower story of the attractive old stone building. Charles Carpy, one of the partners, explained what's been going on there:

"All the old floors, ceilings, plumbing and electricity were replaced and new winemaking equipment installed. Our aging is done in 60-gallon French oak barrels with the exception of Johannisberg Riesling, which is aged in 2,300-gallon American oak tanks.

"The majority of our vineyards are located in the Rutherford area, (climate) Region II . . . In all we will have about 550 acres of vineyard producing within a few years . . . Our production started in 1967 with 60 tons of grapes. In 1970 we crushed 285 tons . . . We should reach our ultimate crush in 1972 of about 400 tons."

Freemark Abbey wines now available are Pinot Chardonnay and Johannisberg Riesling, and Cabernet Sauvignon and Pinot Noir, all vintage-dated.

Heitz Wine Cellars, St. Helena

In less than a decade, Joseph E. Heitz built up his winery from what amounted to a modest roadside business to the point where its name is synonymous among connoisseurs with the finest California wines.

To understand the phenomenon, one must know something of Joe Heitz himself. During the war, while he was stationed in California with the Army, he became interested in wine, and after his discharge he enrolled at the University of California at Davis. He graduated in viticulture and enology, and for the next 10 years he worked as a winemaker for many of the state's leading wineries. He taught vit-

iculture and enology at Fresno State College, and has been a wine
judge at the California State Fair for many years. He and his wife,
Alice, constantly taste the wines of the world at their own table and
through their active membership in the Wine and Food Society.

In 1961 the Heitzes decided it was time to risk giving up the security of working for others and, in a move that required determination as well as raw nerve, they purchased a small winery just south
of St. Helena which had been owned by the late Leon Brendel.

Brendel also was an interesting figure in the California wine industry. A member of a family of wine growers, he was born in the
Alsace District of France and studied chemistry in France and Germany. After helping to organize a school for distillers in Switzerland, he went to Mexico at the request of the family of President
Madero and became winemaker and chemist for the Madero winery
and vineyards in the State of Coahuila. Following Repeal he came to
California as a wine consultant. In 1949 he purchased the winery at
St. Helena which he operated until his death, producing only one
wine, a Grignolino marketed, appropriately enough, under the *Only
One* brand.

Joe and Alice Heitz worked literally night and day to establish
their new enterprise. They believed, and still do, that in the heart
of the fine wine country they can use their own taste and knowledge
to select wines from many producers, blending, maturing, bottling
and selling them under their own label. The public obviously agreed,
and by 1964, the Heitzes were in a position to acquire a second winery and a plot of vineyard land in a valley tucked in the foothills
southeast of St. Helena. The "new" winery is a picturesque, two-
story stone structure built in 1898. Heitz fitted it with new equipment and seasoned cooperage and began replanting the vineyards to
top varietals.

"With our new vineyard and winery we . . . have a self-contained
operation," he said, "in which we can plant the varietals we believe
will ultimately yield the best wines, direct the care and training of
the vines ourselves and from the grapes produce the quality of wine
of which the Napa Valley is really capable.

"We will also continue to select other top quality wines and sell them under the *Heitz Cellar* label."

Despite their youth, the Heitz children already are active in the operation of the winery, making it a true family concern.

Heitz Cellar wines are as follows:

RED: Barbera, Burgundy, Cabernet Sauvignon (Vintage and Non-Vintage), Grignolino, Pinot Noir (Vintage), Ruby Cabernet (Vintage);

WHITE: Chablis, Chardonnay (Vintage), Johannisberg Riesling (Vintage), Pinot Blanc (Vintage).

Also featured are *"Cellar Treasure"* Tawny Port, a Dry Sherry, *Brut* and Extra Dry Champagne and Grignolino Rosé and Malvasia Bianca.

Hanns Kornell Champagne Cellars, St. Helena

Hanns Kornell, a hard working and determined personality, represents the third generation of a family known in Germany since 1848 for their superior wines and champagnes. He attended agricultural college and worked in vineyards and wineries, acquiring experience in France and Italy as well as in his native country. With him as with every true vintner one can say that wine has always run in his blood.

When political conditions made it impossible for Hanns Kornell to remain in Germany he chose America as his new home. In 1940 he hitchhiked to California with $2.00 in his pocket but with determination in his heart. He worked at Fountaingrove in Santa Rosa, then a famous vineyard and winery. He also worked for the Gibson Wine Company in Cincinnati, Ohio, and for the American Wine Company in St. Louis, Missouri, at that time producers of the well known Cook's Champagne, where he was the winemaker and later became production manager.

His great ambition was to manage his own winery and this he accomplished in 1952 when he leased a winery in Sonoma from the Sonoma Wine Company, renaming it Hanns Kornell Cellars. By hard work and a strong inner drive he made his venture a success, so

much so that in 1958 he was able to purchase the famous old Larkmead Winery in St. Helena from Italian Swiss Colony. He had come
a long way in eighteen years, from two dollars to being the proud
owner of his own winery. 1958 was very special for Hanns Kornell
for in that year also he married Marilouise Rossini whose grandfather had homesteaded in St. Helena.

While table wines, including Cabernet and Riesling, and aperitif
and dessert wines are available under the *Kornell Cellars* label the
winery's accent is on the production of bottle fermented sparkling
wines. These are carefully made, aged and bottled under Hanns
Kornell's personal and untiring supervision. They include *Sehr
Trocken* (German for extremely dry), *Brut, Extra Dry, Sec,* Pink
(Rosé) Champagne as well as *Muscadelle du Bordelais* and Sparkling Burgundy, all marketed under the *Hanns Kornell* "Third Generation" brand. Of these the *Brut* Champagne is particularly outstanding.

Charles Krug Winery (C. Mondavi & Sons), St. Helena

This firm, now run by the Mondavi family, is the worthy successor to Charles Krug, a great figure in the development of the California wine industry.

Charles Krug was born in Trendelburg, Prussia, in 1825 and emigrated to America as a young man. He returned to his fatherland to
take part in the democratic uprising of 1848 and on the failure of that
movement returned to the United States for good. He came to California and devoted his energies to a study of viticulture with the aim
of establishing his own winery and vineyards. He worked for General Vallejo and Colonel Haraszthy and became convinced of the
desirability of planting European grape varieties. In 1858 he purchased some acreage of his own and made viticultural history by
producing, from the grapes of John Patchett of Napa, some 1200
gallons of wine with a small cider press. This was the first wine
obtained in Napa County by modern methods. The press is pre-
served at the Krug Ranch today, a treasured memento of its founder.

Krug built his original winery at St. Helena in 1861. The fame of his wines spread throughout the country and beyond. By 1880 the Krug Ranch was considered one of the most beautiful and productive in the Napa Valley and Krug himself was well established as a leader of the wine industry. Such men as Carl Wente and the Beringer brothers worked for him and obtained valuable experience. After the death of Charles Krug in 1894 the Ranch was purchased by his close friend and admirer, James K. Moffitt, who used it as a country home. The winery and vineyards were leased until Prohibition forced them into a dormant period.

When Repeal came the Moffitt family was willing to sell the Ranch but only to a winemaking family capable of reviving the fame and prestige of the Krug wines. With a feeling of accomplishing this purpose the property was sold, in 1943, to Cesare Mondavi and his sons Robert and Peter.

Cesare Mondavi came to America from Ancona, Italy and his, too, is the story of successful enterprise. He first went to work in the ore mines of Minnesota. There he was chosen by a group of Italian home winemakers to select and buy grapes for them in California. He came to stay, engaging in the wine-grape shipping business expanding later to include other fruit. After Repeal he entered the winemaking field, first producing dessert type wines at the Acampo Winery in Lodi. Later he began to produce dry table wines at the Sunny St. Helena Winery in St. Helena. Anxious to concentrate on the production of premium wines the Mondavi family found in the Krug Ranch the means to achieve their goal. Having built up the business with the help of his sons to the present renewed fame of the Krug wines Cesare died in 1959 at the age of 76.

Following his death, Cesare's sons, Peter and Robert, continued to operate the winery. Both graduated from Stanford University and both studied viticulture and enology under University of California scientists. Robert left the family firm to establish his own winery at Oakville in 1966, and Peter now administers Charles Krug as vice president, while their mother, Mrs. Rosa Mondavi, retains the title of president.

Since 1943 the Mondavis have renovated the Krug plant at great expense, modernizing the winery and cellars and re-equipping the buildings. In the vineyards the older wines were gradually replaced and always with the finer varietals. A new glass-lined tank and bottling room were added. These glass-lined tanks, in essence huge bottles, can hold approximately 1,375,000 gallons of wine. The purpose is to be able to bottle the wines when they have received the necessary wood age. It has always been the opinion of the Mondavis that just as much damage can be done to the wine if it is allowed to remain in the wood too long as there would be if it were taken out too soon.

In addition to the glass-lined tanks a new method of bottling has been instituted with certain technical advantages making for better wines. Both these innovations are big steps forward insuring maximum quality.

The main accent of the Krug-Mondavi production is on premium table wines although a few aperitif and dessert wines, including a Tinta Madeira Port, are matured and bottled at the winery to round out the line. A number of less expensive wines are marketed under the *CK* and *Mondavi Vineyards* labels (not to be confused with *Robert Mondavi* wines).

Charles Krug remains the featured brand* for the premium wines. The usual generic table wines are produced; the list of the varietals follows:

RED: Cabernet Sauvignon, Gamay, Pinot Noir and Mountain Zinfandel;

WHITE: Dry Semillon, Sweet Semillon, Sweet Sauvignon Blanc, White Pinot (from 70-75% Chenin blanc and 30-25% Pinot blanc grapes) on the sweet side, Chenin Blanc (from 100% Chenin blanc grapes) on the dry side, Pinot Chardonnay, Traminer, Gewurztraminer, Sylvaner, Grey Riesling and Johannisberger Riesling.

The winery also produces a Riesling, a Vin Rosé (from the Gamay grape) and Moscato Canelli, a lightly sweet Muscat.

* No connection with the Krug Champagne of France.

The Mondavis publish an informative and popular quarterly "Uncorked and poured from time to time by Charles Krug Winery" entitled *Bottles and Bins,* Francis L. Gould, Editor. It gives news about the winery, about the wine industry in general and supplies some very useful and tasty recipes.

Louis M. Martini, St. Helena

The wines produced by Louis Martini rate among the finest of California. Born in Pietra Ligure on the Italian Riviera, Louis M. Martini came to San Francisco as a boy and first assisted his father Agostino Martini, in the latter's mussels, clams and fish business. In 1906, the year of the earthquake, the decision was made to enter the wine making field. A small plant was built in San Francisco, some forty by seventy-five feet, the modest forerunner of the modern and imposing Louis Martini winery in St. Helena of today.

Louis Martini returned to Italy to study winemaking and then returned to California to practice the knowledge he had acquired. He worked for various winemakers, including the famous Secundo Guasti, founder of the Italian Vineyard Company at Guasti. Later Louis Martini built a winery and distillery at Kingsburg in southern San Joaquin Valley for the production of sweet wines and brandy. His ambition, however, had always been directed toward producing premium quality table wines. When he sold his Kingsburg plant for a good price he settled in St. Helena to fulfill his ambition, armed with the necessary know-how, drive and capital.

The St. Helena winery was built in 1933 and Louis Martini successively acquired three vineyard complexes. The Villa del Rey or St. Helena vineyard is located on light, well drained soil along the Mayacamas foothills near St. Helena and is planted mainly to Cabernet Sauvignon, Gamay, Johannisberg Riesling and Chenin blanc. The Napa, or La Loma vineyard, part of the former Rancho Rincon de los Carneros, lies on the rolling, gravelly slopes of the southern end of the Mayacamas range, southwest of the town of Napa. It specializes in Cabernet Sauvignon, Pinot noir and Zinfandel vines.

Most famous, however, is the vineyard formerly called Goldstein, planted in the early eighteen eighties and by Martini renamed Monte Rosso after its red volcanic soil. It is situated at an altitude of over 1000 feet on the crest of the Mayacamas mountains dividing Napa and Sonoma counties. In this cool climate wine grape varieties attain top quality. The Monte Rosso vines include Cabernet Sauvignon, Barbera, Zinfandel in the reds and White Riesling, Gewurztraminer, Sylvaner, Chardonnay, Folle blanche and Semillon in the whites. The wines produced from these grapes are truly "Mountain Wines" and usually carry that designation on the label.

In the early 1960's three additional ranches were added to the Martini holdings. One, on the Russian River bench south of Healdsburg in Sonoma County, was planted predominantly to Pinot noir, Chardonnay, Cabernet Sauvignon, Merlot, Malbec and Gamay. A second, in the Carneros District south of Napa, has been planted entirely to Pinot noir. The third is in Chiles Valley five miles east of St. Helena (at an elevation of 900 feet).

Louis M. Martini is now chairman of the board of the corporation. His son, Louis P. Martini, has replaced him as president. A grandson, Michael Martini, is studying enology and will take an active interest in the business, as will his brother, Peter.

Wines are marketed under the *Louis M. Martini* brand and include the following varietal table wines, all vintage:

RED: Cabernet Sauvignon available in especially fine years as Cabernet Sauvignon Special Selection, Mountain Pinot Noir (available also in magnums), Mountain Barbera, Mountain Zinfandel;

WHITE: Johannisberg Riesling, Mountain Gewurztraminer, Mountain Sylvaner (from the Franken Riesling or Sylvaner grape), Mountain Folle Blanche, Mountain Riesling (from Sylvaner grapes), Mountain Dry Chenin Blanc, Mountain Pinot Chardonnay;

ROSÉ: Mountain Gamay Rosé (from Gamay grape), Mountain Vin Rosé.

Generic table wines are also produced: Mountain Red Wine,

Mountain Claret, Mountain Chianti and Mountain Burgundy in the reds and Mountain White Wine, Mountain Rhine Wine, Mountain Chablis and Mountain Dry Sauternes in the whites.

Three aperitif and dessert wines are available: Pale Dry Sherry (very pale and very dry, of the *Fino* type and aged according to the Solera system), Cream Sherry, Tawny Port (limited quantity only).

Not generally known is that Louis Martini also produces a slightly effervescent wine, Moscato Amabile, made from the Muscat of Alexandria grape, light, delicate and quite sweet. It can only be obtained directly from the winery and should be stored in the refrigerator and consumed early to avoid spoiling.

Also available only from the winery direct are small quantities of very special vintage table wines, the vintages varying naturally as time progresses. This gourmet listing of Martini's "Private Reserve and Special Selection Wines" will include: Cabernet Sauvignon, Pinot Noir, Zinfandel, Barbera, Johannisberg Riesling, Pinot Chardonnay, Gewurztraminer. In each case the vintage year is indicated as well as the year in which the wine was bottled.

Nichelini Vineyards, St. Helena

When Anton Nichelini established his winery in 1890 in the Chiles Valley southeast of St. Helena, he brought years of experience to his new venture. A native of Switzerland, he went to France at an early age to learn the art of winemaking, and he worked for one of California's largest wineries after immigrating to the United States.

Nichelini Vineyards always has been a family affair. It was operated after 1933 by Anton's son William, and since the latter's death in 1959, by Anton's grandson, James. A great-grandson, James Jr., already works in the vineyard.

James Nichelini Sr. had been making wine since he was 17 years old. Although he has replanted much of the vineyard and has started an expansion program at the winery, the original plant built by his grandfather still is in use. Today, the Nichelini property yields Cabernet Sauvignon, Gamay, Petite Sirah, Zinfandel, Chenin blanc, Flora, Palomino and Sauvignon vert grapes.

Table wines available under the *Nichelini Vineyard* label are as follows:

RED: Burgundy, Cabernet, Sauvignon, Gamay, Zinfandel;

WHITE: Chablis, Chenin Blanc, Sauvignon Vert;

ROSÉ: Vin Rosé (of Zinfandel grapes).

In addition, Nichelini Vineyards markets a Dry Sherry and a Port.

Stony Hill Vineyard, St. Helena

Some seven hundred feet above the floor of the Napa Valley, on the steep hillsides between Spring and Diamond mountains, lies the Stony Hill Vineyard, the name of which speaks for itself. The vineyard, some 38 acres, is planted mainly to four varieties, all white: Chardonnay, Pinot blanc, White Riesling and Gewurztraminer.

Frederick H. McCrea, now retired from his position as vice president and manager of the San Francisco office of McCann-Erickson, Inc., an internationally known advertising agency, long had the ambition to see what he could do about producing good wines in small quantities. He purchased the Stony Hill property in 1943 and built a small but modern winery in 1951. The wine is fermented in small cooperage, and much of it is held two years before sale.

Only a small portion of the grapes grown are used by McCrea himself. Chardonnay and Gewurztraminer are bottled under the *Stony Hill* brand, carrying the vintage on the label as well as the Napa Valley appellation of origin.

Souverain Cellars, St. Helena

It is on the slopes of Howell Mountain, overlooking the Upper Napa Valley from the East that the ranch and vineyards founded by J. Leland (Lee) Stewart are to be found.

It was in 1943 that Lee Stewart, always appreciative of fine wines, decided to enter the wine growing and winemaking fields himself. Headed for Ukiah, Mendocino County, he happened to detour by way of St. Helena and falling in love with the area he found himself purchasing the old Peter Stark place above the Silverado Trail. Gradually he modernized and enlarged the winery and replanted the vineyards. His aim is to combine the best traditions of the European wine grower with the most modern California methods and in this he has handsomely succeeded. An artistic feature of the winery is the beautifully carved entrance door depicting a vintage scene, the work of Merrill Abbott.

What had first started out as a hobby soon became a steady business, running in the black after much work and overcoming many difficulties. In 1970 it was purchased by a consortium of Napa Valley residents. The accent remains on the production of premium table wines.

Before selling Lee Stewart made many further improvements to the winery. The storage space was considerably enlarged, there is now a complete laboratory and office, a refrigeration unit has been added for cold fermentation as well as a new fermentation room including a press imported from Germany.

Rosé (from Grenache) is produced at the winery and *Los Amigos* Sherry Sack* and Tinta Madeira Port are marketed but the winery's main business is concerned with its premium table wines all from the Napa Valley as indicated on the labeling.

Spring Mountain Vineyards, St. Helena

It can be predicted safely that this winery, located in a little-known but highly-regarded vineyard area near St. Helena, will gain more notoriety as time goes on.

Michael Robbins, a San Francisco businessman and dedicated enophile, established his cellars in a restored Victorian house on 170 acres. Although only a fraction is planted now, nearly 50 acres are expected to be in production by 1975, with Cabernet Sauvignon, Pinot Noir and Chardonnay heading the list. His first wine, a Sauvignon Blanc, was a fine beginning.

* Once produced by Los Amigos Vineyards of Mission San Jose, now no longer in existence.

Beaulieu Vineyard, Rutherford

It was just before the turn of the century that a young Frenchman, Georges de Latour, came to California, desirous of producing table wines comparable in quality and character to the finer ones of his native France. He had heard much about California's favorable climate and soil and he came to see for himself. He stemmed from a family well known in both the Bordeaux and Burgundy regions and was already familiar with many of the problems of viticulture and of the difficult art of winemaking. He was, besides, gifted with an exceptionally fine taster's palate, an attribute of primary importance to all those engaged in the wine business, and especially in the producing end of it.

Georges de Latour traveled through California searching for the ideal location suited to his purpose and found what he sought in the Rutherford area in the Napa Valley. It was here, in 1900, that he founded the Beaulieu* estate and vineyards, as he named them so appropriately.

For some forty years Georges de Latour devoted his energies to the production of the finest wines the favored climate and soil of the Napa Valley were capable of yielding. He proved himself eminently successful in his endeavor and established a solid reputation for the Beaulieu wines throughout the United States and abroad.

During Prohibition the winery continued to operate, producing sacramental wines, to which a part of the Beaulieu industry is still actively devoted. Beaulieu is one of the few wineries in California where the accent in wines and wine production is very distinctly inspired by the French taste; the whole atmosphere is that of *"la belle France,"* completely at home in the Napa Valley.

After the death of Georges de Latour in 1940, Madame de Latour presided over Beaulieu in her husband's place. Known to so many for her grace and charm, she had become the *"grande dame"* of California viticulture. With her demise, in 1951, another great figure had passed on.

* Meaning Beautiful Place.

Today Beaulieu is owned by Heublein Inc., the huge firm that has bought so many of California's premium wineries.

The reputation of Beaulieu's wines has progressed with the times, their quality the result of a happy blending between the traditional subtleties of French taste and know-how in the modern California manner. To this philosophy fully subscribes French-trained André Tchelistcheff, who joined Beaulieu in 1938 and is the production manager in charge of the winery and vineyards. He skillfully adapts New World techniques of quality-wine production to his store of Old World winemaking experience.

There are five Beaulieu vineyards, two of them located at Rutherford, two at Oakville and one south of these near San Francisco Bay, each being planted with the grape varieties best suited to its particular soil and location.

The brand name under which all wines are marketed is *Beaulieu Vineyard*. As some have difficulty in pronouncing the name, the labels also carry the letters *B V,* and it is by this name that the wines are also widely known. All table wines are labeled with the Napa Valley appellation of origin and with the exception of Beaurosé and Grenache Rosé are estate bottled. The back label indicates exactly from which grapes the wine has been made, the varietals being mostly 100%.

The *Beaulieu (B V)* table wines include:

RED: Cabernet Sauvignon and Cabernet Sauvignon Private Reserve (with extra years of bottle age), Beaumont Pinot Noir, Burgundy (from Gamay, Pinot Noir, Petite Sirah and Mondeuse of Savoy grapes);

WHITE: Chateau Beaulieu (from Sauvignon blanc grapes with a touch of Muscadelle du Bordelais), Beaufort Pinot Chardonnay, Beauclair Johannisberg Riesling (White Riesling), Dry Sauternes (from Semillon and Sauvignon blanc grapes), Sweet Sauternes (from Semillon, Sauvignon blanc and a touch of Muscadelle du Bordelais), Chablis (from Chenin blanc, Melon de Bourgogne and French Colombard grapes), Riesling (from Franken Riesling or Sylvaner grapes);

ROSÉ: Beaurosé (from Cabernet Sauvignon, Gamay and Mondeuse grapes), Grenache Rosé (from that grape only).

In recent years Beaulieu has started to produce and market sparkling wines, all bottle fermented. These are the *Beaulieu (B V)* Champagnes, *Brut* and *Extra Dry* and the *Rouge* or Sparkling Burgundy.

Beaulieu also markets aperitif and dessert wines matured in small oak casks including the *B V* Sherries (Pale Dry, regular, medium dry, and Cream), *B V* Port and *B V* Muscat de Frontignan.

All of the varietal table wines of Beaulieu and their sparkling wines carry the vintage year on the labeling and many an older *B V* vintage table wine has become a connoisseur's item.

Franciscan Vineyards, Rutherford

A new and ambitious development in the Napa Valley, Franciscan Vineyards expected to sell its first 50,000 cases of wine in 1972.

Organized in October, 1971, with business executives Bernard D. Bruttig and Charles R. Dilling as president and vice president-secretary respectively, the company obtained an option on 164 acres bordered by the Napa River at Rutherford. The founders hoped to plant 150 acres and expected the vines to begin producing by 1975. At the same time they planned construction of a $750,000 winery complex which was to reach a capacity of 1.3 million gallons within five years.

The winemaker for the new firm is Roy Raymond Sr. and the enologist is Walter Raymond, both formerly of Beringer at St. Helena.

The company projected a complete line of aperitif and dessert, generic and varietal table wines and sparkling wines, all under the *Franciscan Vineyards* label. Its national sales program was to include direct sales, mail order and a tasting room at the winery opening in the spring of 1972.

Inglenook Vineyard Company, Rutherford

The great vinecovered stone winery of Inglenook lies in Rutherford, right in the heart of the Napa Valley. Beaulieu (see there) is its immediate neighbor.

Founder of Inglenook was that colorful Finnish seafarer, fur trader and wine grower, Captain Niebaum.

Gustave Ferdinand Nybom (later Americanized to Niebaum) was born in Helsinki, Finland, in 1842, at that time under Russian domination. He went to sea as a boy and received his master's papers when only nineteen. Two years later he had his own command and in 1864 sailed for Alaska, then also part of the Russian Empire.

For three years he ranged Alaska, the Aleutian Chain of Islands and the Asiatic shore as far as Kamchatka, bartering for furs and acquainting himself thoroughly with the region. Negotiations by the United States for the purchase of Alaska had been started and Captain Niebaum realized that America would have economic as well as political interests in the territory. He made full use of his opportunities and amassed a vast collection of seal skins and other valuable furs. When the sale of Alaska to the United States became an accomplished fact in March 1867 Captain Niebaum lost no time in loading his precious furs aboard a ship, bound for San Francisco. He was no more than twenty-six when he sailed through the Golden Gate, the owner of a cargo worth well over half a million dollars.

Captain Niebaum's knowledge of the seal habitat was invaluable to the Alaska Commercial Company, organized to obtain exclusive fur sealing rights in the Alaskan waters, and he became their youngest partner. The company proved so successful that it paid the United States Government considerably more in rights than the total cost of the Alaskan purchase.

The Captain was now ready for a less rigorous mode of life and as Mrs. Niebaum did not share his love for the sea he turned his thoughts to the land and to an enterprise that both could enjoy.

On various trips that he had made to Europe on behalf of the

Alaskan company he had become increasingly interested in viticulture and winemaking. He had visited many of the European wine growing districts and had collected a large number of books on the subject. His hobby finally became his life's destiny. With enough time and money to accomplish his purpose he decided to attempt producing in California wines comparable to Europe's finest.

After a thorough search for the most suitable location Captain Niebaum purchased in 1879 a portion of the old Mexican Caymus Rancho grant, extending from Rutherford up to the slopes of Mount St. John, highest peak of the Mayacamas range. The property had already been called Inglenook (Scottish for fireside corner) by the former owner, W. C. Watson. The name appealed to Niebaum and he retained it.

Captain Niebaum devoted the following years to planning, building and planting. Further trips to the wine growing regions of Europe were made where he studied every aspect of viticulture. Cuttings of the choicest wine grape varieties were shipped home. At Inglenook he established his vineyards with the utmost care and always with due regard to the beauty of Nature. The cellars and winery were built according to the most modern specifications. Inglenook had became Captain Niebaum's ship and the vineyards his sea.

When Captain Niebaum died in 1908 Inglenook was inherited by his widow. John Daniel, the husband of Mrs. Niebaum's niece, ably directed operations for her until the advent of Prohibition. His knowledge was passed on to his son, John Daniel, Jr., who was in charge of the winery and vineyards from Repeal until he sold out to United Vintners in 1964. United became part of the Heublein empire in 1969.

Inglenook was the first winery to label many of the better known varietals as such, pioneered such wines as White Pinot,* Red Pinot,† Charbono‡ and claims to have been the first producer of Vin Rosé in California, launching it in 1935.

* Chenin Blanc, see white varietal table wines chapter.
† Pinot St. George, see red varietal table wines chapter.
‡ *Ibid.*

The following Napa Valley table wines are available under the *Inglenook* label, all marked with their vintage year:

RED: Cabernet Sauvignon, Pinot Noir, Red Pinot (Pinot St. George), Gamay and Charbono;

WHITE: Semillon (moderately sweet), Pinot Chardonnay, White Pinot (Chenin Blanc or Pineau de la Loire), Riesling (Franken Riesling or Sylvaner) and Traminer;

ROSÉ: Navalle Rosé (from Gamay grapes and named after the stream that runs through the property).

In addition, since the sale to United Vintners, a new line of less expensive generics, called District Vintage Wines (not estate bottled), has been introduced. These include Burgundy, Zinfandel, Chablis and Rhine. California Grenache Rosé has been added, along with five vintage appetizer and dessert wines, three Sherries and two Ports.

F. J. Miller & Co., Rutherford

It may seem unusual that this winery is included in this book, because the owner isn't exactly in the wine business. But he considers himself somewhat of a missionary for a new process for carbonating wines, and, as such, he has become one of the best known and most controversial figures in the industry.

F. Justin Miller is an Englishman who ran a plantation in the West Indies before he came to California. He studied food technology at Davis with the idea of returning to Trinidad, but after graduating in 1951 he decided to settle in the Napa Valley instead to work on his theories about carbonation. He learned that carbon dioxide introduced into liquids while they are quiescent rather than disturbed (conventional methods of artificial carbonation require violent agitation) result in greater stability. In other words, the bubbles last longer.

Miller buys and matures wine before he puts it through his "Millerway" process, which he patented in 1960. First, the wine is filtered and drawn into a pressure tank from which each bottle is filled. The bottles are placed open in small, individual cylinders, air is pumped out to prevent oxidation and carbon dioxide is introduced into the headspace at a pressure of 150 pounds per square inch. The cylinders are opened after 12 hours, the bottles are stoppered and the product is carbonated wine with about 50 pounds of pressure—roughly the same as naturally fermented Champagne. The difference is that the effervescence lasts longer after the bottle is opened, up to *sixteen days* if it is not shaken, and remains at a constant temperature.

Miller sees many other advantages to the process. Wines can be matured carefully, brought to their peak and then carbonated in a few hours. Millerway wines lack the characteristic flavor of Champagne, which he calls "yeasty" and which he believes many Americans don't enjoy. However, he adds, if a winemaker wanted the Champagne flavor, it can be achieved with the process.

Miller is not primarily interested in selling *F. J. Miller* wines, although they are available in small quantities from the winery. He is concerned with selling the process, which has not been widely accepted. He blames traditionists and the federal tax regulations which prohibit labeling machine carbonated wines as "sparkling." To back up his belief that wine producers would buy the process if they could so label their products, he has initiated legal action against the government to win that right.

The wines carbonated through the Millerway technique are sound and interesting, with true varietal flavor.

Robert Mondavi Winery, Oakville

One of the newest and most attractive wineries in the Napa Valley is operated by Robert Mondavi, who established it in 1966.

The Mondavi family has been associated for two generations with winemaking in California, and since 1943, has owned the Charles Krug winery at St. Helena (see there). Following the death of Cesare Mondavi in 1959, Krug was operated by his sons, Peter and Robert Mondavi. Now Robert, with the assistance of his own son, Mike, and in partnership with Sicks' Rainier Brewing Co. of Seattle,

Wash., is, in the words of one associate, "working to produce the finest Napa Valley wines possible" on his own.

The winery, designed by architect Cliff May and landscaped by Thomas Church, was built with a neo-colonial motif, complete with 15th Century Spanish doors. The antique-looking adobe-colored exterior of the building conceals a modern winery where technology is married to tradition. Double-walled stainless steel tanks which allow controlled temperature fermentation contrast with small, European-made oak casks.

In 1968, the winery was expanded to accommodate as many as 400 to 500 guests for specially arranged tastings, luncheons, concerts and other events.

The following table wines (all varietals) are available under the *Robert Mondavi Winery* brand:

RED: Cabernet Sauvignon, Gamay, Pinot Noir, Zinfandel;

WHITE: Chardonnay, Chenin Blanc, Fume Blanc (a dry wine of Sauvignon blanc grapes named after the Pouilly-Fume of France's upper Loire Valley), Riesling (a blend of Sylvaner and Grey Riesling), Sauvignon Blanc (lightly sweet), Traiminer;

ROSÉ: Gamay Rosé.

Oakville Vineyards, Oakville

This organization was incorporated in 1969 as a descendent of Carmel Valley Wine Associates, a small company formed the year earlier to produce and market fine wines. The head of both companies is W. E. van Löben Sels, an agricultural economics graduate of the University of California and a successful Bay Area businessman. The winemaker, Peter Karl Heinz Becker, comes from a German family that has been making wine over 300 years. He joined the Carmel Valley-Oakville Vineyards venture after 11 years as plant manager and winemaker at Almaden's Cienga winery near Hollister. Others active in the day-to-day operation of the new company are Mrs. Jean van Löben Sels, the president's wife; California historian V. Aubrey Neasham and William M. Weeks.

Oakville Vineyards has launched an ambitious and costly program of development and expansion, beginning at its winery and tasting room in Oakville. Two other vineyards are located north and south of the nearby town of Yountville, and all told the corporation controls 265 acres planted mostly to prime varieties.

Oakville Vineyards varietals will reach the market containing nearly 100 per cent of the named grapes. From all reports they will include outstanding wines.

Napa County—Lower Napa Valley

The Christian Brothers (Mont La Salle Vineyards), Napa

The Mont La Salle Vineyards and Novitiate of The Christian Brothers are located high in the hills of the southwestern part of Napa County in the so-called Napa Redwoods district, some eight miles northwest from the town of Napa.

The "Brothers of the Christian Schools" as The Christian Brothers are officially called, form a congregation of the Roman Catholic Church, dedicated to the education of young men and boys. The order was founded in 1680 at Reims, France, by Jean Baptiste de la Salle, for the purpose of educating the underprivileged. Its headquarters are in Rome. Although not priests, the Brothers lead dedicated lives, having taken the vows of poverty, chastity and obedience.

The Christian Brothers first came to the United States before the middle of the nineteenth century. At present they operate one hundred and seventy-four institutes of learning in the country, such as Manhattan College in New York City, La Salle Military Academy on Long Island, St. Mel's High School in Chicago, Christian Brothers College in St. Louis and St. Mary's College at Moraga near Oakland in California.

Mont La Salle at Napa is The Christian Brother's Novitiate for California and the Western States. Here young men are trained for the work of the congregation while a school is maintained for boys of high school age and a home for Brothers who have retired after a lifetime of service. Here also the Brothers proudly follow their wine making tradition, a heritage dating back many centuries.

In California The Christian Brothers started making wine at Martinez in 1882, at first for their own use, then for Sacramental use and later, with the growing demand by lay circles, for the public. The Brothers are sole owners of the wineries and use all net profits for the maintenance of their Novitiate at Mont La Salle, where young men are trained to carry on the educational work of the Order, and to help support the operation of various schools in the San Francisco Province.

Four members of the Order, Brother U. Gregory, president and general manager, Brother Timothy, vice president and chief winemaker, Brother Frederick, assistant to the president, and Brother Justin, Viticulturist, personally supervise the operation of the wineries at Mont La Salle and at St. Helena both in Napa County and at Reedley in Fresno County.

The Brothers produce table and Sacramental wines in the old stone winery built at Mont La Salle in 1903. Wines requiring long term aging are brought to the St. Helena Aging and Champagne Cellars, an old stone landmark once known as the largest stone winery in the world. After reaching their peak of maturity here in the wood they are then returned to Mont La Salle for bottling and bottle aging. The St. Helena Cellars are also the headquarters for the Brothers' champagne production. Sparkling wines are produced by the Charmat process in sixteen glistening stainless steel tanks which enable the Brothers to maintain complete scientific control. The Mt. Tivy winery is given over to the production of The Christian Brothers aperitif and dessert wines and brandy.

All the Brothers' products are marked under *The Christian Brothers* brand with the exception of their Altar wines which bear the *Mont La Salle* label. In 1967, the Brothers abandoned the heavy, ornate "cathedral" bottles which had been their trademark and began marketing wines in more traditionally shaped containers.

The regular types of generic table wines and of aperitif and dessert wines, including vermouths, are available as well as (bulk fermented) sparkling wines and of course the well known *Christian Brothers* Brandy.

Among the table wines are a number of varietals, including:

RED: Cabernet Sauvignon, Gamay Noir, Pinot Noir, Pinot St. George, Zinfandel;

WHITE: Sauvignon Blanc (Dry and Sweet), Pinot Chardonnay, Chenin Blanc, Johannisberg Riesling, and Grey Riesling. A light muscat, is also marketed, called Chateau La Salle. *Pineau de la Loire* is a Chenin Blanc.

Mayacamas Vineyards, Napa

Some 2,000 feet high in the Mayacamas Mountains in the Lokoya district, near the top of Mt. Veeder, an extinct volcano, lies this small winery enthusiastically devoted to the finer things of life. According to local authorities Mayacamas means "Howl of the Mountain Lion" and is derived from the language of the Lokoya tribe of Indians who once inhabited the region.

Mayacamas Vineyards was founded by Jack F. M. and Mary Catherine Taylor. A graduate of Cambridge University in England and the former president of the Shell Development Company, Jack Taylor was for 20 years Mayacamas' sole wine maker, vineyard manager, viticulturist and chemist.

The Taylors became wine growers for the simple reason that they had always liked fine wines. They decided, in 1941, on the Mt. Veeder property because of its beautiful setting, its excellent grape growing location and because there was a winery and distillery there, dating back to 1889 and known for a time as Mount Veeder Vineyards.

The old vineyards were all ripped out, terraced at great expense, fenced to keep out the deer who are connoisseurs of the better grapes, and replanted mostly to Chardonnay, yielding the wine in which the Taylors specialized with justified pride.

In 1958, in an effort to meet the growing demand for their wines, the Taylors formed a corporation, offering the shares directly to their customers as part of their determination to retain the "family" feeling of the enterprise. With the capital thus acquired they worked towards doubling their small capacity, still keeping in the category of small wineries.

In 1961 the Taylors turned the management of Mayacamas over to younger people, and in 1968 control was acquired by Robert Travers, who is carrying on in the best traditions. An investment banker who apprenticed himself to Joe Heitz in St. Helena to learn the wine trade, Travers, along with winemaker Robert Sessions and vineyard manager Michael Clancy, has expanded the storage and has added new vineyards of Cabernet Sauvignon and Chardonnay, which will become specialties.

For years Mayacamas wines were available only at the winery on an exclusive basis. However, expansion has made it possible for them to be sold through stores and restaurants.

The two featured brands are *Mayacamas* and *Lokoya,* the former being reserved for wines made from grapes either wholly or partly grown on the estate and produced at the winery while the latter is used for wines, specially selected on account of their high quality.

The *Mayacamas* wines are all 100% of the variety named on the label.

Wines bearing the *Mayacamas* label are the Chardonnay, Chenin Blanc, Gamay, Zinfandel Rosé and Cabernet Sauvignon.

Under the *Lokoya* brand the following wines are marketed: Red and White Table wine, Dry and Sweet Vermouth, and (bottle fermented) Champagne and Sparkling Burgundy.

SOLANO COUNTY

Cadenasso Wine Company, Fairfield

Here at Fairfield, Solano County, in the Suisun district is to be found the Cadenasso Winery, producer of some fine table wines, including Grey Riesling, Grignolino, Pinot Noir and Zinfandel. It is a family owned enterprise now operated by Frank Cadenasso, his wife

Joan and their four children. The featured brands are *Cadenasso* and *Solano Vineyards*.

The Cadenasso Wine Company was founded in 1906 when Giovanni Cadenasso, who had immigrated from Italy shortly before, started his own vineyard and winery on the Rutherford Ranch in Green Valley, north of Cordelia. In 1916 Giovanni moved to Fairfield and planted vineyards on the site where the Solano County Hospital now stands. With Prohibition, wine making came to an end and the winery was dismantled and Giovanni sold his property to the County. Wine making, however, remained in his blood. So undaunted, he started a third vineyard in 1926, aided by his son Frank, across the road from his former location. This he did in the firm conviction that Prohibition would be repealed. He had judged rightly and when Repeal came his vineyards were prospering once more.

Giovanni Cadenasso has now passed on and so Frank is now the owner, winemaker and vineyard manager, assisted, as stated above, by his family. His uncle Giuseppe Cadenasso, Giovanni's brother, was the well known painter who taught art at Mills College.

C. *ALAMEDA—CONTRA COSTA DISTRICT*

This district, as famous in its own way as that of Napa-Solano, consists of a number of separate wine producing areas.

Celebrated throughout the country and beyond is Alameda County's Livermore Valley, home of unsurpassed California wines of the Sauterne types. Some red table wine is also produced as are sparkling wines and aperitif or dessert wines of great merit. The Livermore Valley, actually not so much a valley as a wide basin, comprises two neighboring wine growing areas, the famed vineyards centering around the town of Livermore, with their gravelly vineyards, and separated from them only by some low hills to the west, the sector around Pleasanton.

Second only in importance to the Livermore Valley is southern Alameda with its wine growing center of Mission San Jose.

Contra Costa County is best known for its table wines, grown in the shadow of Mt. Diablo, which rises so majestically to a height of nearly four thousand feet.

ALAMEDA COUNTY—THE LIVERMORE VALLEY

Concannon Vineyard, Livermore

An old firm with a famous name, well known for its premium wines. The main accent is on the production of white table wines as is to be expected in the heart of the Livermore Valley district.

James Concannon, the founder, was born in the Aran Islands, County Galway, Ireland in 1847 and as a youth determined to carve out a career for himself in what he called "that shining land across the seas."

He saved up enough money for his passage and after holding various jobs in the East could afford to be married by 1874 and a year later brought his bride to San Francisco.

In the West James Concannon found full opportunity to apply his energy and resourcefulness. He pioneered the rubber stamp business on the Pacific Coast and included Mexico in his travels. In Mexico City he criticized the then prevailing sanitary conditions in no uncertain terms with the result that the famed dictator of Mexico, Porfirio Diaz, sent for him. Diaz took a liking to the forthright and energetic young man and entrusted him with full authority to remedy the situation.

The rubber printing stamp, however, was what made Concannon's fortune. By 1883 he had amassed sufficient capital to settle down with his family and farm. It was at the advice of his friend, the colorful Archbishop of San Francisco, Joseph S. Alemany, that James Concannon decided to produce wines for religious use and that he purchased, in the Livermore Valley, a suitable ranch from

Horace Overacher, a homesteader. Concannon's success as a vine-yardist and winemaker became rapidly established and the high traditions he set have been carried on down continuously to this day.

After James Concannon died in 1911, operation of the winery was continued by his five sons; James, John, Robert, Thomas and Joseph. During Prohibition, while only Sacramental wine was produced, management fell to "Captain Joe" Concannon (so named because of his service as a Cavalry officer during the 1916–1918 expedition against Pancho Villa in Mexico). Eventually, "Captain Joe" and his wife acquired full ownership and he remained as president until his death in 1965. His widow still lives on the ranch, which has been expanded to include more than 300 acres. The other four brothers have since passed away.

The third generation of Concannons now operates the winery, with Joseph Jr. as president and James as vice president, winemaker and chemist. Shares in the corporation remain with members of the immediate family.

Concannon Vineyard has undergone an extensive replanting program in the past decade, with future plans placing emphasis on Johannisberg Riesling in the whites and Petite Sirah and Cabernet Sauvignon in the reds. Champagnes, for sale only at the winery, were added to the line in 1958 to commemorate the 75th year of the firm.

Concannon Vineyard is the brand featured and the following table wines are marketed, all with the Livermore Valley designation of origin on the label:

> WHITE: Sauvignon Blanc, Johannisberg Riesling, Dry Sauterne (dry Semillon), Chateau Concannon (sweet Semillon), Chablis, Moselle, White Dinner Wine;
> RED: Petite Sirah (the first bottled in California), Cabernet Sauvignon (limited bottling, Vintage), Red Dinner Wine, Burgundy;
> ROSÉ: Vin Rosé (slightly sweet) and Zinfandel Rosé (exceedingly dry).

Aperitif and dessert wines are also marketed including a Vintage Muscat de Frontignan (18% alcohol), an exceptional sweet dessert wine with a pronounced but delicate perfume and flavor, and *Prelude* Dry Sherry, one of the best of the "new" 17% Sherries.

The *Concannon* Champagnes (see also above) are bottle fermented and produced from the Concannon Livermore Vineyards. They include a *Brut,* one of Californias driest with a sugar content of less than 1% and an *Extra Dry,* in the medium range of dryness.

Wente Bros., Livermore

Bearing one of the greatest names in the California wine industry, the Wente family produces some of the finest white table wines of the country, notably of the sauterne and white burgundy varieties.

Carl H. Wente, the founder of the firm, was a native of Hanover, Germany, and came to this country in 1880. He received his first experience in California wine making under the personal supervision of Charles Krug, the great pioneer viticulturist of Napa Valley. Carl Wente soon branched out for himself and purchased, late in the fall of 1883, some vineyards in the Livermore Valley south of the town of Livermore. On this land the original Wente winery still stands.

From the beginning Carl Wente specialized in the production of the finest quality table wines, for which he found a ready market and at prices considerably higher than the average at that time. Both the Semillon and Sauvignon blanc grapes of the Sauternes region in France soon proved themselves to be particularly well suited to the Livermore soil and climate, and so, later on, did the Chardonnay of white burgundy and champagne fame.

Gradually the Wente holdings were extended, first by the founder and later on by his sons, Ernest and Herman Wente. An important acquisition was that of the neighboring El Mocho vineyards. When that highly regarded wine growing pioneer of the Livermore Valley, Louis Mel, retired at an advanced age, he sold his treasured El Mocho property to the Wentes. Mrs. Mel-de-Bire was a friend of the contemporary Marquis de Lur-Saluces, owner of the world renowned Château d'Yquem in Sauternes, near Bordeaux in France, and when Charles Wetmore, as delegate of the California Vinicultural Society and the founder of Cresta Blanca, was charged with obtaining cuttings of the finest European vine varieties, she gave him a letter of introduction to the proprietor of Yquem. Wetmore returned with cuttings of the Semillon, Sauvignon blanc, and Muscadelle du Bordelais vines from the vineyards of Château d'Yquem itself and naturally gave some to Louis Mel, who propagated them in his El Mocho vineyards. When the present Marquis de Lur-Saluces visits California, he never fails to call on the Wentes to enquire how his "California Yquem children" are faring and to taste with appreciation what California is capable of producing in the way of sauternes.

Karl L. Wente, grandson of the founder, is now president and general manager of the Wente operation. He is fortunate in having the wise counsel of his father, Ernest, who remains the farmer and wine grower, and in having the promise of continuity in his two sons, Eric and Philip. Herman Wente—unassuming and simple but regarded by many as the greatest winemaker in California—died in 1961.

Much of the soil of the Wente vineyards is alluvial deposit, washed down from the hills to the east and containing considerable heavy gravel, well suited to the finer grape varieties that like to mature the hard way. The sight of these gravelly vineyards is a perpetual source of wonderment to the novice.

The grapes are picked, variety by variety, at the peak of ripeness for wine making.

The Wentes are optimistic as to the future and are planting more vineyards to the fine varieties so suited to the Livermore area. The winery, too, has been modernized with a new building, new bottling equipment and air-conditioning for the best protection of their wines.

Under pressure from residential development in the Livermore Valley, the Wentes explored and tested other California soils and climates until they found what they believe is an ideal location for new vineyards in Arroyo Seco Canyon at the end of Carmel Valley Road 15 miles from the Pacific in Monterey County. There, in rocky soil warmed by day and cooled by valley breezes at night, they have planted varieties such as Pinot noir, Gamay, Pinot blanc, Chenin blanc and White and Grey Riesling.

The famous specialties of the Wentes are their white table wines, unsurpassed in California.

Most of the varietals carry the vintage date. *Only* table wines are produced, all marketed under the *Wente Bros.* brand. Two standard wines are marketed, a red and a white under the *Valle de Oro* label, the romantic name which the Spaniards gave to the Livermore Valley.

The following *Wente Bros.* wines are available:

In the Sauterne style bottle: Dry Semillon and Sauvignon Blanc. Chateau Wente, produced from a blend of Semillon and Sauvignon blanc with the addition of a little Muscadelle du Bordelais and as fine a sweet wine of the Sauterne order as can be produced in California is only available in the Western part of the United States as the amount of the wine is limited.

In the Rhine wine style bottle: Grey Riesling.

In the Burgundy style bottle: Pinot Chardonnay, Pinot Blanc and Chablis. A new addition has been *Le Blanc de Blancs,* a blend of Chenin blanc and Ugni blanc grapes.

Although the Wente winery is best known for its white table wines it also produces Burgundy, Gamay Beaujolais, Pinot Noir and a very popular Rosé made predominantly from the Gamay grape with a small addition of Pinot noir.

Villa Armando Winery, Pleasanton

This operation passed into its present ownership in 1962 when the old Garatti holdings at Pleasanton were purchased by Anthony D. Scotto of New York, a member of a family which has grown and made wines for more than a century in Italy and the United States.

The original winery was founded in 1902 by Frank Garatti, a native of the Italian province of Lombardy. He planted the vineyards and ran the company until his death in 1948. His son-in-law, F. W.

Brenner, took over until he, too, died in 1960. Under the Villa Armando Winery ownership Robert F. Diana, well known in California wine circles, became general manager.

Most Villa Armando wines are shipped to the Metropolitan New York area, but an increasing amount is sold in California stores and through a retail outlet at the winery. A new tasting room and expanded wine touring facilities were to have been completed by 1971.

Several generics are available under the *Villa Armando* brand, including Chablis, Sauterne, Burgundy, Chianti, Rubinello, Orobianco and Vino Rustico. Varietals offered are Barbera, Pinot Noir, Zinfandel, Malvasia Bianca and Semillon.

Ruby Hill Vineyard Co., Pleasanton

Ruby Hill is a beautiful wine growing ranch with tall and stately palms lining the driveway to the residence, with vineyards stretching out on all sides. The great winery, which lies beyond the residence, was built in 1887 by John Crellen, later succeeded by C. L. Crellen, and by whose family name the estate was known for many years. In 1921 the property was purchased by Ernest Ferrario, the present owner and wine maker.

Ernest Ferrario was born near Lake Como in Italy and came to this country in 1901, first settling in New York and then in California. He worked on the railroads in San Raphael and in the brickyards in San Francisco. Accustomed to wine in his native country, he has always been interested in wine making, but what made him go into the wine business in California, according to his own story, was Prohibition. The reason for this had to do with the high prices obtainable for grapes grown for home wine makers, as allowed by law. During the dry period he also made wine for medicinal and sacramental purposes.

Ferrario sells most of his production to other wineries. At the same time Ruby Hill is a popular place for those who like to buy their wines at the winery itself, be it by the case or barrel.

Under the *Ruby Hill* brand premium table wines are available as well as Sauterne and Burgundy.

SOUTHERN ALAMEDA COUNTY
(Mission San Jose District)

Llords & Elwood Winery, Mission San Jose

Most wineries are founded by winemakers who, because of the necessities of commerce, eventually become salesmen of at least their own brands. With the growing firm of Llords & Elwood the situation was reversed. By the time J. H. (Mike) Elwood decided to become a winemaker, he already had devoted nearly 20 years to becoming one of Southern California's best known retailers of high quality wines and spirits.

A native Californian, Elwood left the outdoor advertising business with Repeal and opened a small package store in the Los Angeles area. The company expanded, catering to customers who knew and appreciated fine wines and spirits, and by the time he and his attractive wife, Irene, sold it in 1961 to devote their full attention to the Llords & Elwood Winery, the chain consisted of stores in West Hollywood, Beverly Hills and Brentwood. They kept the firm's name (Llords had been added when Elwood acquired a store by that name), and today it is associated with one of California's leading lines of premium wines.

The Elwoods have traveled widely, and their knowledge of the finest wines of Europe reveals itself in their products.

The Llords & Elwood Winery was started with the cooperation and encouragement of Rudolf Weibel of Weibel Champagne Vineyards (see there). In 1955 the Elwoods built their winery adjacent to the Weibel facilities in Fremont's Mission San Jose District about 40 miles southeast of San Francisco. The first wines produced were two Sherries and a Port which entered the retail market in the fall of 1961. Since that time seven other wines have been added—five table varietals, an excellent bulk fermented Champagne and another Sherry. A bottle-fermented Champagne was to replace the original in 1972.

Elwood is his own winemaker, buying most of his grapes from growers throughout the state and relying on his highly educated palate in the process of the vintage, blending and aging. Winery superintendent Sal Vicari divides his time between the Fremont plant and two Llords & Elwood cellars in San Jose. Elwood has become treasurer of the family corporation, Mrs. Elwood is secretary and their son, Richard, is president with offices in Los Angeles, thus freeing the parents for the extensive travel essential to solidly establish a relatively new brand.

In 1969 Richard Elwood also became president and general manager of L & E Vineyards Company, which developed 127 acres of prime land in the Napa Valley. The showplace vineyard, planted only to selected Pinot noir and Chardonnay rootstocks, was to be in full bearing by 1974.

Llords & Elwood wines are now sold in leading retail outlets and can be found in fine restaurants. An interesting feature of the line is the use of proprietary names for varietal wines. For instance, their Johannisberg Riesling carries the name "Castle Magic" and the Pinot Noir is called "Velvet Hill."

The other wines:

RED: Cabernet Sauvignon;

WHITE: The Rare Chardonnay;

ROSÉ: Rosé of Cabernet (made with Cabernet Sauvignon grapes);

SHERRY: Great Day D-r-ry Sherry, Dry Wit Sherry, The Judge's Secret Cream Sherry;

PORT: Ancient Proverb Port.

Weibel Champagne Vineyards (Weibel, Inc.), Mission San Jose

Weibel Champagne Vineyards, founded in 1939, produces champagnes, table and aperitif and dessert wines which have established an excellent reputation for themselves. It is a family enterprise, owned and operated by Frederick E. Weibel, president and general manager. Fred Weibel Jr. is executive vice president.

The Weibels are natives of Münsingen, Canton of Bern, Switzerland. The late Rudolf Weibel had been engaged in the wine and champagne business in his native country and in France and came to the United States as an importer of wines and brandies in 1934. He traveled all over the country and, when he came to California, observed its climate and soil, the fine wine grapes which could be grown and the quality of wines it was possible to produce. Comparing them type by type with those of Europe, he made up his mind to emigrate to the United States and devote himself in California to the production of the finest wines that could be made. So he came to this country in 1936 for good, accompanied by his son Frederick.

Production of high quality champagne was the main ambition of the Weibels and for that reason the enterprise was called Weibel Champagne Vineyards, a name to which they have done full justice.

The Weibels first settled in San Francisco making champagne from purchased wines while looking around for a suitable winery and vineyard property. This they found in their ranch and winery near Mission San Jose* on the Warm Springs site of the old Leland Stanford Winery. Late in September 1958 the State Historical Landmarks Advisory Committee held formal dedication ceremonies on the Weibel property, erecting a landmark inscribed "Leland Stanford Winery—Founded 1869" in the presence of some 500 officials and other guests.

The site was famous long before the coming of the Spanish Conquistadores. Indians used to frequent the warm springs to benefit by their healing capacities. It was a dedicated area and no tribal wars were fought in the vicinity.

A Spanish land grant gave a vast territory, including the Mission, to the Higuera family in 1836 who named it "Rancho del Agua Caliente" on account of its warm springs. In 1860 Clement Colombet bought a large acreage of the Rancho upon which he built a fashion-

* Founded by Father Junipero Serra in 1797.

able resort, the Warm Springs Hotel, surrounded by vineyards. The Hotel flourished until it was wrecked by the earthquake of 1868.

The following year Leland Stanford, railroad builder, Governor, Senator, and founder of Stanford University, bought a square mile of land at Warm Springs. His brother, Josiah, planted some 350 acres of vines there and built a winery with a capacity of some 500,000 gallons, later adding a brandy distillery. Warm Springs did a flourishing business, large quantities of "Stanford" wine being sold. Leland Stanford deeded the property to his brother Josiah, and encouraged by the latter's success in the wine business and affirming his belief that California was the world's best wine country he embarked on his famous wine growing project at Vina, Tehama County, an enterprise which lasted well into the twentieth century. The Weibels purchased their ranch in 1945 and devoted the next few years to replanting the vineyards and modernizing the winery. They have steadily been expanding their business capturing also the Eastern markets.

Weibel is the featured brand for all products sold directly to the public.

The bottle fermented *Weibel* Champagnes include Chardonnay *Brut, Brut, Extra Dry, Sec,* Pink Champagne and Sparkling Burgundy. Other Sparkling Wines produced are their Crackling Rosé and Moscato Spumante (Sparkling Muscat) and a trademarked specialty, Crackling Duck.

Both generic and varietal table wines are available, the latter including:

WHITE: Chardonnay, Johannisberg Riesling, Chenin Blanc, Green Hungarian and Grey Riesling;

RED: Pinot Noir, Cabernet Sauvignon, Royalty, Gamay Beaujolais and Zinfandel;

ROSÉ: Grenache Rosé.

Estate Bottled Vintage Chardonnay and Pinot Noir are available in limited quantities.

Aperitif and dessert wines, including Dry and Sweet Vermouth, are produced and include "Dry Bin" Cocktail Flor Sherry (dry), "Gallery" Flor Sherry (medium), "Amberina" Cream Flor Sherry (sweet), "Governor's Rare" Solera Port and "Memento" Cream of Black Muscat.

The *Weibel* Brandy is a fairly recent addition but not so the wine called "Tangor" with a flavor of tangerines, the winery claiming to be the originator of the "Natural Flavored Wines" (see Chapter VIII).

NORTHERN ALAMEDA COUNTY

Bynum Winery, Albany

When Davis Bynum finally opened his own winery in 1965, it was the culmination of a long dream. A newspaperman who spent 15 years working for the San Francisco *Chronicle,* he acquired his appreciation of fine wines from his father, Lindley Bynum, author of "California Wines and How to Enjoy Them."

The elder Bynum, a California historian associated with the University of California Libraries at Berkeley and Los Angeles before becoming a U.C. executive, was a wine judge at many California State and Los Angeles County Fairs. Following his retirement he moved to St. Helena and grew wine grapes until his death in 1965.

Dave wanted to establish his winery in the urban area to give his clients an opportunity to see all of the operations—trucking in grapes, crushing, fermenting, racking, bottling, etc. However, as the reputation of Davis Bynum wines grew, the Albany plant became too small and inconvenient. In 1968, he started moving all of his production, storage and bottling facilities to a new premises on Lodi Lane in St. Helena. The original winery was retained, and a new tasting room and retail outlet was planned.

The Bynum Winery is truly a family operation, with Dave as the winemaker. When his wife, Dorothy, isn't helping in the winery she handles much of the bookeeping, and their two children, Hampton and Susan, do what work is left—which is quite a bit.

The brands available are *Davis Bynum Private Reserve* for limited bottlings of exceptionally fine wines, *Davis Bynum* for premium wines and *Barefoot Bynum,* a unique and colorful label used for bulk wines. Several generics are sold in addition to the following varietals:

RED: Cabernet Sauvignon, Pinot Noir, Ruby Cabernet, Zinfandel;

WHITE: Chenin Blanc, Muscadelle, Dry Semillon, Franken Riesling (of Sylvaner grapes), Grey Riesling, Johannisberg Riesling;

ROSÉ: Grenache Rosé, Cabernet Rosé (of Cabernet Sauvignon grapes) and Zinfandel Rosé.

The Bynum Winery offers two Ports and four Sherries, including an excellent seven-year-old Amber Dry Sherry.

CONTRA COSTA COUNTRY

J. E. Digardi Winery, Martinez

This winery was founded in 1886 by Frank Digardi, a native of Sicily, where cousins still own vineyards in the neighborhood of Palermo. Frank Digardi planted vineyards on the slopes of Mount Diablo and later acquired and developed other vineyard properties in the county.

The enterprise was carried on by Joseph E. (Joe) Digardi, son of the founder and a well known personality in the wine industry, and by his family. The business has devolved to his son, Francis. Family vineyards in the Clayton Valley lying in the shadow of Mount Diablo and in the Vine Hill area south of Martinez have been taken for residential development.

Red table wines are featured with *Digardi* the brand for wines of premium quality. *Diablo Valley* is the brand for dessert and bulk wines.

Conrad Viano Winery, Martinez

The Viano family vineyards have been nestled in a small valley almost within sight of Suisun Bay since Prohibition. Theirs is the only significant vineyard land left in Contra Costa County, in an area once so rich in grapes it was called Vine Hill. Despite the tremendous pressure of residential development and the high taxation which accompanies it, the Vianos have steadfastly resisted the bulldozer and are, in fact, replanting to expensive varietals.

The vineyards were established by the late Clement Viano, scion of a centuries-old winemaking family from Italy's Piedmont region. In 1946 the present winery was established and it has been expanded several times since. At the present time there are three generations involved in the business including the four children of young Clement Viano, the grandson of the founder and a 1958 graduate in viticulture of the University of California at Davis. Clement operates the winery with his father, Conrad (from whom it gets its name), and his mother.

Clement Viano is an enthusiastic and tireless winemaker who has modernized the plant and, in keeping with the motto he dreamed up ("It's the Grapes") experiments with both red and white varietals.

Viano is the brand for bulk Zinfandel, Burgundy, Sauterne and Vin Rosé. The *Viano Private Stock* label is reserved for the following premium generics and varietals:

RED: Barbera, Burgundy, Cabernet Sauvignon, Gamay, Zinfandel;
WHITE: Chablis, Grey Riesling;
ROSÉ: Grenache Rosé and Zinfandel Rosé.

In addition Tokay, Sherry, Port and Muscatel are available.

D. *SAN FRANCISCO*

California Wine Association, Burlingame

This famous old company has a long history dating back to 1884 when a number of California's well known wineries joined to form the original California Wine Association. Membership has varied over the years but the company has always played an important part in the California wine industry. In 1929 it was reorganized as Fruit Industries, Ltd. but reverted back to its former name in 1951.

For many years A. R. Morrow was the dominant figure of the firm. The memory of this "grand old man" of California viticulture will always be cherished and his name is prepetuated in one of the company's familiar brands. Edwin R. Mettler is president of California Wine Association, L. S. Durrell is chairman of the board, W. Perelli-Minetti is executive vice president, Mario Perelli-Minetti is a vice president, and Gordon Nelson is winemaker and director of quality control.

California Wine Association is composed of a number of cooperative and other wineries which are located in the major wine growing districts of California and to which a large number of grape growers contribute their grapes. In this manner the company can obtain the various types of wine where it is most advantageous to do so with regard to regional suitability and quality.

The main offices of the company are located on the San Francisco Peninsula. The Association completed a large combination warehouse and bottling plant in Lodi in 1959 while its producing plants expanded their facilities.

The member wineries are the following: Cherokee Vineyard Association at Acampo, Rancho del Oso Winery, at Lodi, and A. Perelli-Minetti & Sons at Delano. In addition wines are obtained on a selective basis from another dozen wineries.

California Wine Association is one of the largest producers in the state and its wines and brandies enjoy a national distribution, the brands varying somewhat according to region and locality.

Table wines and aperitif and dessert wines, including vermouths, as well as sparkling wines and brandy are produced and marketed.

Ambassador is the featured brand for the premium wines of all types while *Eleven Cellars, Greystone* and *F.I.* are other well known brands of the company. *A. R. Morrow* and *Aristocrat* are the labels restricted to brandy. "Red Rooster" is the name given to the natural flavored type wine marketed by the Association.

E. SANTA CLARA—SANTA CRUZ AND SAN BENITO DISTRICT

The neighboring counties of Santa Clara and Santa Cruz, with the Santa Cruz Mountains forming the border between the two, are usually grouped together as one wine growing district. Extensions of this district include the wine growing areas in San Benito County and in San Luis Obispo County.

Santa Clara County can be divided into three wine growing areas, spreading west and east from the Santa Clara Valley floor to the adjoining hills and mountains.

West of the Santa Clara Valley, in the foothills, lies Los Gatos, and higher yet, in the hills beyond, Saratoga, together forming the Los Gatos-Saratoga area. Here are the homes of some of the finest table wines and champagnes of California, while fine aperitif or dessert wines are also produced.

To the east of San Jose lies the hillside Evergreen area with its vineyards stretching onto the slopes of Mt. Hamilton. From this section hail a number of superior table wines.

The southern part of Santa Clara County and of its valley is noted for an important winery section, centering around Morgan Hill, San Martin and Gilroy, with good wines of all types being produced from the neighboring hillsides. Many a sound "country" table wine also is produced in the small wineries, run mostly by Americans of Italian descent, in the section west of Gilroy up towards the Hecker Pass and in the Uvas area.

Santa Cruz County is equally noteworthy for its wines. Some excellent table wines are produced above Felton and at Soquel. Besides there are scattered vineyard areas in the county including Vinehill, towards Los Gatos, Bonny Doon, southwest of Ben Lomond, Boulder Creek, north of that Scottish-named elevation, and Laurel area in the mountains towards the Santa Clara County line, and the Casserly section, up towards Mt. Madonna.

San Benito yields some fine table wines, while San Luis Obispo County, where Paderewski once grew his wine grapes and almonds, is noted for its hillside table wines, especially Zinfandel.

SANTA CLARA VALLEY—LOS GATOS, SARATOGA AREA

Almadén Vineyards, Los Gatos

About midway between Los Gatos and the former quicksilver mining village of New Almadén* and some five miles south of San Jose are to be found the winery and domain of Almadén, overlooking the undulating hills towards Loma Prieta and the Mountains that separate Santa Clara and Santa Cruz Counties. Here some of the finest California champagnes are produced as well as table and aperitif and dessert wines of great merit.

The founder of Almadén was Etienne Thée, a farmer from Bordeaux in France who is said to have been lured to California by the Gold Rush. In any case he devoted himself to less elusive and more permanent pursuits, grape growing and wine making. To this end he purchased from the Guadalajara pioneer José Augustin Narvaez part of the old Rancho San Juan Bautista, securing for himself a fertile tract of land along the creek called Guadalupe River. Here in 1847 he built his home, that still stands today, on a high knoll with its sweeping view of the valley and of the mountains beyond.

Thée was soon joined in his enterprise by a neighbor and compatriot, Charles Lefranc, said to have been a tailor in Passy, the suburb of Paris. The vineyards were planted in 1852 cuttings of choice vines imported from the districts of Champagne, Bordeaux, Burgundy and the Rhône Valley. Lefranc married Thée's daughter, Adèle, and eventually inherited his father-in-law's property. He prospered together with his vineyards and by the end of the eighteen seventies

---

* So named by the Spaniards after the quicksilver mines of Almadén in the Province of Ciudad Real, New Castile, Spain.

could boast that they contained more vines than any other in the county and, what was more important, that his wines rated with the best. The finest cooperage was imported from France around Cape Horn, some of it in use down to the present. Many were the famous guests who enjoyed Lefranc's hospitality, among whom are said to have been numbered Admiral Farragut and Generals Sherman, Halleck and Ulysses S. Grant.

The French influence and atmosphere were dominant at Almadén and this tradition was strengthened when Lefranc hired a young Burgundian to help in the office and winery. This was Paul Masson who was to make his own name great in the California wine industry and followed precedent by marrying Lefranc's daughter, Louise. Eventually Masson became associated with his father-in-law in the production and merchandising of champagnes and table wines in a jointly owned business, Lefranc-Masson. Later he established himself on his own property in the hills above Saratoga (see Paul Masson Vineyards).

Almadén (the property was given the district name of Almadén in 1941) was inherited by Charles Lefranc's son Henry and after the latter's death in 1909 was held in trust for the family until it was sold to Charles Jones. With the advent of Prohibition Almadén entered a dormant period as far as wine making is concerned.

In 1941 Louis A. Benoist, well known San Francisco businessman and president of the Lawrence Warehouse Company, national field warehousing concern, purchased the property at the advice of the noted wine authority Frank Schoonmaker. Oliver J. Goulet, one of the foremost experts in the field, was engaged as winemaker and plant manager. In this capacity he was ably assisted after 1954 by A. C. (Al) Huntsinger, now winemaker and production manager.

The winery and other buildings were renovated and the original vineyards were brought into shape. Additional acreage was acquired, planted to the finest varietals.

In 1967 Almadén was taken over by National Distillers which operates it as a subsidiary. B. C. Ohlandt is chairman of the board, and the president is William A. Dieppe.

Recent winery expansions include a new champagne cellar and a sherry room featuring six Soleras, making Almadén's Solera operation one of the most modern and largest in the country. A huge binning cellar for bottle aging red table wines houses inventories of Cabernet Sauvignon and Pinot Noir with the purpose of aging red wines at least two years in glass before placing them on the market.

Almadén's acreage was increased in 1955 by the purchase of the Sykes Ranch at Paicines near Hollister in San Benito County in the area of the Pinnacles where the legendary bandit Joaquin Murietta hid out during his brief and bloody career. The rolling hills on which cattle grazed have been transformed into extended mountain vineyards to assure adequate supply and reserve of choice wine variety grapes to meet the steadily increasing demand for the finer varietal wines. Here also, at Paicines, a crushing operation and a distillery, for brandy production, are located.

San Benito County, in the area around Hollister, has for long had an enviable reputation for yielding premium wines. Its best known wine enterprise, Valliant Vineyards, is now also operated by Almadén. The Paicines and Valliant Vineyards, total more than 4,000 acres.

Today, white wines are made at Paicines where Almadén, reputedly the first winery to bring them from Germany, has a battery of Willmes presses. Wines are giving their initial aging and then are shipped to Los Gatos for further aging and bottling. Red wines and Ports are produced at the Cienega winery located along the foothills of a parallel valley to Paicines. Built in the 1880's by Hollister mayor William Palmtag, the winery stands astride the San Andreas Fault and has attracted seismologists from all over the world to see the cleft in the floor kept open by earth tremors. Cienega houses the largest cellars in the world for table wines and Sherries, with more than 35,000 small oak barrels in its interior.

Another important vineyard belonging to Almadén is located at Pleasanton in the celebrated Livermore Valley white table wine district.

Almadén Vineyards produces a complete selection of premium wines marketing them under the *Almadén* label.

The sparkling wines (bottle fermented) number the *Blanc de Blancs,* made from Chardonnay, *Brut, Extra Dry* (medium) as well as Rosé (Pink) Champagne and the inevitable Sparkling Burgundy. Le Domaine is the brand of cheaper sparkling wines.

Table wines include generic types such as the Mountain Reds and Whites and Estate-Bottled Vintage varietals as well of course as the varietals, the latter listing reading:

RED: Cabernet Sauvignon, Pinot Noir, Gamay Beaujolais, Zinfandel;

WHITE: Dry Semillon, Pinot Chardonnay, Pinot Blanc, Johannisberg Riesling, Gewurztraminer, Sylvaner, Grey Riesling, Chenin Blanc and Sauvignon Blanc.

ROSÉ: Grenache Rosé and Mountain Nectar Vin Rosé.

The three *Almadén* Sherries are of the *flor* type and blended and aged according to the Solera system: Solera Cocktail (dry), Solera Golden (medium) and Solera Cream (sweet). The Solera Ruby and Tawny Ports are also blended and aged in the same manner. *Almadén* Vermouth comes in Pale Triple Dry and Sweet types. In 1952 the winery launched its "Centennial Brandy" to celebrate the 100th year of its establishment. Although *Almadén* Brandy still is sold, it is now a separate label of National Distillers.

David Bruce, Los Gatos

A San Jose physician who spent eight years studying wine making and vineyard techniques before taking the plunge, David Bruce purchased his vineyard property high in the mountains above Los Gatos in 1961. Assisted by his family he planted nearly 25 acres of Chardonnay, White Riesling, Cabernet Sauvignon and Pinot Noir. Although the original winery wasn't built until 1964, it rapidly was outgrown and construction of a new 6,000 square foot concrete building was completed in 1968. An innovator who designs much of his own equipment, Bruce plans some new processing techniques when the new winery is in operation.

To help meet the growing demand for his wines, Bruce purchased another 15 acres in the Santa Cruz Mountains, and other future vineyard acquisitions are planned. Although *David Bruce* wines have been available primarily from the winery, they will appear in selected retail outlets. Offered (all Vintage and 100% varietal) are Chardonnay, Pinot Noir, Cabernet Sauvignon and Zinfandel. White Riesling, Grenache and Petite Sirah were to be added.

Novitiate of Los Gatos, Los Gatos

In the hills above Los Gatos one finds the magnificently situated Seminary of the Sacred Heart Novitiate of the Society of Jesus and its beautiful vineyards. Here young men begin their training for missionary work in the Orient, for teaching positions in schools operated by the Jesuits in California, or for parochial duties in some of the dioceses along the West Coast.

Since its founding in 1888 the Novitiate has maintained the tradition for producing fine altar wines in strict accordance with the Canon Law of the Roman Catholic Church. Once the needs for sacramental wines is met, the remainder of the production is made available to the public through commercial channels.

The Jesuit Fathers and Brothers have full charge of the production of the wines. The novices and junior students help pick most of the grapes each fall. Many of the vines were imported from France, as were the muscats from the Montpellier region near the Mediterranean.

Father Harry T. Corcoran, S.J., is the president of the Novitiate, while Father Henri Charvet, S.J., is vice president and vineyard manager; Father Louis B. Franklin, S.J. is vice president and general manager; Brother Lee Williams, S.J., is the winemaker and Father James E. Ransford is the chemist.

The Novitiate's Altar Wines are only available to the clergy. They are similar or identical to the wines marketed for the public (see below) but are in each case labeled with a distinctive name, appropriate to the particular wine.

A listing of the Novitiate's Altar Wines follows:

"Manresa" (Red Burgundy), "Villa Joseph" (Sauterne), "Vin Doré" (Sweet Sauterne), "San Carlos" (Chablis), "Santa Rosa" (Grenache Rosé);

"Villa Maria" (medium dry sherry), "San Pedro" (Port), "San Ignacio" (Tokay), "L'Admirable" (Angelica), "Guadalupe" (Muscat de Frontignan), "San Jose" (Red Muscat).

Available to the public under the *Novitiate* brand are the following table and aperitif and dessert wines, all in the premium class:

Table wines: Burgundy, Sauterne and Chablis in the generics and Cabernet Sauvignon, Pinot Noir, Zinfandel, Pinot Blanc, Chenin Blanc and Grenache Rosé in the varietals.

Dry Semillon and Sauvignon Blanc were formerly produced separately but these are now used for reasons of economy in the Dry Sauterne and Chateau Novitiate production, the latter a sweet wine of the Sauterne type. White Riesling is offered when the vintage warrants.

The Novitiate is also well known throughout the country for its aperitif and dessert wines. These include Sherry, Dry Sherry, *Flor* Sherry, Cocktail Sherry, Port, Angelica, a wonderful Muscat Frontignan and an altogether exceptional dessert wine (used by many as a cordial), the Black Muscat, made entirely from blended vintages of Muscat Hamburg grapes.

Paul Masson Vineyards, Saratoga

A great name in the history of the California wine industry and a national enterprise, started by that famed Frenchman from Burgundy, Paul Masson, the origin of the enterprise dating back to 1852.

Paul Masson came to work for Charles Lefranc at his winery between Los Gatos and New Almadén, eventually marrying his boss's daughter, Louise (see Almadén Vineyards). He became associated with his father-in-law, the firm being called Lefranc-Masson. After Lefranc's death it bore the name of Paul Masson alone.

In the 1880's Paul Masson established himself on a property in the Santa Cruz Mountains above Saratoga where the soil and climate were eminently suited to the growing of the finer wine grape varieties and planted his vineyards to cuttings to the choicest imported vines. The winery Paul Masson built on this mountain property was partly destroyed by the 1906 earthquake but was rebuilt by him in the following years using some of the sandstone from the old St. Joseph's Church in San Jose which had been destroyed in the same disaster. He also obtained from the ruins of the Church a 12th century Romanesque portal which had originally come from Spain.

Paul Masson made his name forever famous by producing champagnes and table wines of the highest quality. For over half a century he worked in his steeply sloping mountain vineyards and in his wine cellars establishing a great name for his wines and becoming somewhat of a legendary figure himself. For several years he was a Viticultural Commissioner for the State of California. He made frequent trips to his native France, purchasing additional vine cuttings and the latest in winery equipment. One of the firm's earliest awards for fine wines was made at the Paris exhibition of 1900. In 1936 Paul Masson retired from his vineyards and passed away four years later, a greatly respected personality and true modern pioneer of the best that can be produced in California wines.

Before he retired Paul Masson had sold his vineyards and winery to Martin Ray. A disastrous fire occurred in 1941, wrecking the winery and causing great losses but Martin Ray rebuilt both the winery and his business. Two years later he sold the enterprise to Joseph E. Seagram's, the distillers, later establishing another domain of his own even higher up in the mountains (see Martin Ray). Seagram's operated the Masson winery and vineyards only a short while, being succeeded in 1945 by a company in which Alfred Fromm and the late Franz Sichel were the partners. Both the Fromm and Sichel families have been in the wine industry for a great number of years, the former for five generations and the latter for seven. Otto Meyer is now president of the firm. Leo A. Berti, qualified by his specialized education and by years of experience in the California wine industry, is vice president in charge of production. Marketing has been taken over by Browne Vintners Co.

In recent years the Paul Masson firm has extended its vineyard holdings through the purchase of the San Ysidro Ranch near Gilroy which was planted to varietal wines under the supervision of University of California viticultural specialists. In 1962–63, the 1,000-acre Paul Masson Pinnacles Vineyard was planted in Monterey County. Another 500 acres was begun in 1968. Recent plantings will raise the total to 5,000 acres.

In 1959 the firm opened the Paul Masson Champagne Cellars in Saratoga. In view of the historic mountain vineyards the new Champagne Cellars consolidate the bottling, packaging and shipping facilities for the entire Paul Masson line, including the brandy. In a building designed to practice generations old traditions in modern surroundings visitors have the opportunity to observe all wine aging and champagne making operations and to taste the various types of wines produced by Paul Masson. The building is of eye catching modernity with a roof consisting of six huge wood arches. It contains 225,000 square feet and what with the "Champagne" fountain 67 feet high set in a 9,000 square foot reflecting pool and a reception rotunda featuring a spiral ramp to the visitors gallery it is a most impressive sight.

The new winery is located some three miles to the east of the famous old Paul Masson winery, previously the focal point for visitors. It is here that a natural bowl forms the lovely setting for summer Sunday concerts featuring many a famous artist and it is here on the terrace overlooking the Santa Clara Valley from an imposing height that many an *al fresco* meal has been enjoyed while quaffing some fine Paul Masson table wine or champagne.

Paul Masson Vineyards produces and markets both generic and

varietal table wines, sparkling wines, aperitif and dessert wines including vermouth, as well as brandies, all under the *Paul Masson* label.

The varietal table wines include:

RED: Cabernet Sauvignon, Pinot Noir, Gamay Beaujolais;

WHITE: Pinot Chardonnay, Pinot Blanc, Chateau Masson (Sweet Semillon), Emerald Dry (Emerald Riesling) and Johannisberg Riesling.

There is a *Paul Masson* Vin Rosé Sec. Proprietary wines include Baroque and Rubion (reds) and Rhine Castle (white).

The regular types of aperitif and dessert wines are marketed both in fifths and in half-gallons while the Rare Dry Sherry, Rare Cream Sherry and Rare Tawny Port come in heart shaped decanters as does the new Rare Souzao Port. The Vermouths include both a Double Dry and a Sweet type.

Paul Masson Vineyards are especially famous for their Sparkling Wines. These include *Brut* Champagne, available also in Magnums and Jeroboams,* Red Champagne (Triple Red), marketed in the same sizes, Extra Dry Champagne, Pink Champagne and Sparkling Burgundy (Cuvée Rouge), all three available in larger bottles also. Another new wine is Crackling Rosé.

Martin Ray, Saratoga

High above Saratoga Mt. Eden rises steeply to an altitude of some two thousand feet. It is there, on the summit of the mountain, commanding a grandiose view of the whole of the Santa Clara Valley, that Martin Ray devotes his skill to the production of table wines and champagnes comparable to the finest of France.

Born into a farming family of Saratoga, Martin Ray first became a stockbroker, a profession he followed with such success that he was able, at a relatively early age, to start the winemaking career he dearly ambitioned. He had set his heart on Paul Masson's winery

---

* Magnums hold 2 bottles while Jeroboams hold twice again as much.

and vineyards above his native village and in 1936 he accomplished his desire, purchasing them from that great man when the latter retired from his life's work. Desirous of concentrating on the finest varietals exclusively—a field in which he was one of the pioneers— he sold the Paul Masson vineyards and name in 1943 (see Paul Masson Vineyards) but retained the original historic corporation dating back to 1852, amending its name to his own. He then purchased, built and planted his present domain which adjoins his former property but is situated on even loftier heights.

Martin Ray—Rusty as he is known to his friends—has become somewhat of a legendary figure in his lifetime. He is a dynamic, energetic, eccentric and forceful personality, deeply devoted to his art and as profoundly appreciative of truly fine wines as he is impatient with any other. He is not modest when it comes to his wines. His vineyards, planted on the eastern and southern exposures of the mountain slopes, are set out to four varieties only: Pinot noir, Cabernet Sauvignon, White Riesling and Chardonnay. An underground concrete pipe system with strategically located sumps ensures proper drainage during the rainy season and preservation of the top soil. All of the work done in the vineyards as well as in wine making, bottling and shipping is done by Martin Ray and his immediate family or under their immediate supervision. The wines are clarified not by filtering or fining but by racking and decanting and therefore sometimes throw a deposit as do many of the great European vintages.

The *Martin Ray* wines are all 100% varietal and of the best vintage years only. Any wine not measuring up to the highest standards is disposed of and sold in bulk. The policy is to produce and market only the finest and to improve wherever possible, regardless of cost. Production is on a small scale, the wines being destined for gourmets and connoisseurs and for the best restaurants and clubs. It is not surprising that their cost is high.

Martin Ray is ably seconded in many phases of his work, as well as in his eloquent correspondence, by his charming wife, Eleanor. They are wonderful hosts, presiding over repasts that miraculously stretch out into the most unexpected hours, preceded as they are by the quaffing of vintage champagnes and enlivened by sparkling conversation and the finest of table wines.

Most fortunate also is Martin Ray in being able to select as his successor his son, Dr. Peter Martin Ray, an outstanding plant physiologist who is familiar with the great European vineyards, has done considerable research on grape varieties and is an authority on wines as well as winemaking.

All wines are marketed under the *Martin Ray* label.

Table wines available are various vintages of Pinot Noir, Cabernet Sauvignon and Chardonnay selling at case prices ranging from a stiff $96 ($8 per bottle) to an absolutely incredible $600 ($50 per bottle!) for his 1970 Chardonnay *Fruit Mur, Ecrasant!* The following, with descriptions by the Rays, range in price from $180 to $200 per case:

Champagnes

Madame Pinot: a special *blanc de noir* made from the free run juice of the Pinot noir: 1964.

Blanc de Noir: pale-gold champagne uniquely made from Pinot noir without the grapes being crushed. Costliest of Martin Ray champagnes: 1964.

Sang de Pinot: "Blood of the Pinot" produced from the first light pressing of Pinot noir grapes: 1964.

Champagne de Chardonnay: a *blanc de blancs* made 100% from the Chardonnay grape: 1964.

Ridge Vineyards, Cupertino

This is another example of those small California premium wineries which have been started since the war by "non-professional winemakers"—men following the traditions established by Stewart at Souverain, McCrea at Stony Hill and Zellerbach at Hanzell. David R. Bennion, winemaker at Ridge Vineyards and a researcher at Stanford Research Institute, began experimenting with wine after he and three partners purchased a venerable vineyard on the southwest side of Monte Bello Ridge at an altitude of 2,300 feet, a short distance north of the Mt. Eden property of Martin Ray (see there). The partners—Bennion, H. D. Crane, C. A. Rosen and H. M. Zeidler—originally bought the land for speculation, but by 1962 they had decided to establish a bonded winery. Zeidler later sold out to the other three, and R. W. Foster, Carl Djerassi and Alejandro Zaffaroni have since joined the enterprise through capital expansion.

Much of the property was part of the original Monte Bello vineyard, and the winery building dates back to the turn of the century, although its first known use as such was in the 1920's. It passed through many hands until 1948 when William Short acquired it and began upgrading the vineyards to Cabernet Sauvignon and Pinot noir. Following the 1959 purchase, additional plantings were undertaken, and other property has been added to the domain.

All *Ridge Vineyards* wines are Vintage-labeled and unfiltered, which means they may throw a deposit in the manner of the great wines of Europe. Usually available are White Riesling and Chardonnay in the whites, and in the reds, Cabernet Sauvignon, Zinfandel and a blend of Zinfandel and Ruby Cabernet.

Gemello Winery, Mountain View

This small family winery, founded in 1934 by John Gemello is situated right off the busy El Camino Real in Mountain View and produces and markets wines for sale mostly in its flourishing retail outlet on Highway 101. John Gemello born near Asti in Piedmont, Italy, the home of some of Italy's most famous wines, retired in 1944 and Mario Gemello, his son, is now president of the enterprise. John Gemello, it may be noted, once worked in the vineyards of and made wine at the original Monte Bello winery in Cupertino. Little could he have dreamed at that time of the myriads of cars swooshing along El Camino Real in Mountain View and of the enterprise he started, hard to find for those in a hurry but still easy for those who want to locate a small and select winery and retail outlet. In 1969 Louis C. Sarto acquired a one-third interest and took over marketing.

The Gemello Winery specializes in the finer varietal table wines although the usual types of aperitif and dessert wines are also available, purchased and marketed under the *Gemello's* featured label, *Mountain View* being the secondary brand.

The finer varietal table wines are either purchased or produced at the winery and aged in small oak casks or puncheons and include:

RED: Pinot Noir, Gamay, Zinfandel, Barbera and an especially noteworthy Cabernet Sauvignon made from 100% Cabernet Sauvignon grapes and on the average 8 years old, produced from grapes grown in the Saratoga foothills on land once owned by Paul Masson;

WHITE: Pinot Chardonnay (from grapes grown in the Black Mountain area in Santa Clara County) Pinot Blanc (from the Saratoga district), Sylvaner, Grey Riesling and Riesling (a blend);

ROSÉ: Grenache Rosé, Zinfandel Rosé and Cabernet Rosé.

WOODSIDE-PORTOLA VALLEY

Nepenthe Cellars, Portola Valley

As is the case with Woodside Vineyards, the only other winery in San Mateo County, Nepenthe Cellars is just one step removed from the classification of home winery. Bonded in 1967 by George Burtness, a young land development executive at nearby Stanford University, the winery has a permanent staff consisting of Burtness, his wife, Yvonne, and their small daughter, Laura.

Originally a hobby winemaker who began experimenting in 1962, Burtness named his venture after the ancient Greek word for a potion to relieve pain and sorrow. Although he tends a small vineyard, most of his grapes are purchased from growers in the Santa Cruz Mountains and upper Napa Valley.

The principal *Nepenthe Cellars* wines are Cabernet Sauvignon and a full aged Zinfandel made in the fashion of Bordeaux. Others include Pinot Noir, Petite Sirah, Chardonnay, White Riesling and a rosé made from Petite Sirah and Pinot Noir.

Woodside Vineyards, Woodside

Robert Lee Mullen was a teetotaler before he came to California in 1955. On the day he arrived he drank his first glass of wine, and he has been a confirmed enophile ever since.

An executive with a national building materials firm, Mullen and his charming wife were living in Woodside when they made their first wine as amateurs in 1960. By the time they obtained their bond in 1963, they had built another home in the same community, this one equipped with a modern and compact winery-laboratory in a specially-built cellar. Production now averages 1,000 gallons per year.

In collaboration with close friends, the Robert Groetzingers, the Mullens planted most of their small plot to Chardonnay and Pinot noir. On nearby properties, parts of the original Rixford "La Questa Vineyards" founded in 1883 but long since subdivided, they tend two acres of Cabernet Sauvignon. Now, with assistance from scientists at the University of California in Davis and Oakland wine consultant Julius Fessler (and, of course, the neighbors who help with the harvest), *Woodside Vineyards* is in a position to offer two Vintage whites, Chardonnay and Chenin Blanc. Cabernet Sauvignon is sold under the *La Questa* label dating from 1883, and Pinot Noir was to come on the market. The wines, all in the premium class, are sold only from the winery or in Woodside retail outlets.

Mirassou Vineyards, San Jose

The type of operation at Mirassou Vineyards is a unique one, for many years producing varietal table wines and champagne stock of premium quality to be sold in bulk to other wineries. A growing quantity of these wines is bottled and sold to consumers in selected states.

Mirassou Vineyards grow about 90% of the grapes used in the making of their varietal wines and have spent over one hundred years in determining which varieties grow the best and produce the finest wines in the Santa Clara Valley, world renowned for its quality fruit. While the legal minimum requirement for varietal labeling is 51% the varietal wines from Mirassou Vineyards are bottled at nearly 100% from the grapes after which the wines are named.

The enterprise is presently operated by Edmund A. and Norbert C. Mirassou, fourth generation wine growers, and their sons, who are continuing the tradition started in Santa Clara Valley by their great-grandfather Pierre Pellier in 1854. It is located in the rolling hills between the Santa Clara Valley and Mount Hamilton in the district known as Evergreen, where they own 350 acres. Another 50 acres is owned at Gilroy, and a new 300-acre vineyard has been founded near Soledad in Monterey County. Another 650 acres has been planted near Soledad by the fifth generation, which also owns and operates the marketing company.

The following varietal table wines (all vintage) are available to the public under the *Mirassou* label:

WHITE: Chardonnay, Chenin Blanc, Gewurztraminer, White (Johannisberg) Riesling, Sylvaner Riesling, Pinot Blanc and Semillon (dry);

RED: Pinot Noir, Petite Sirah, Cabernet Sauvignon, Gamay Beaujolais and Zinfandel;

ROSÉ: Petite Rosé (made of Petite Sirah).

Sparkling wines (bottle fermented) are also produced and bottled handsomely under the Mirassou Vineyards label. They include Champagne Au Natural, *Brut,* Pink Champagne and Champagne Rouge.

Santa Clara Valley—Morgan Hill and Gilroy-Hecker Pass District

Pedrizetti Winery, Morgan Hill

A classic little country winery, Pedrizetti nonetheless produces a few remarkable (and inexpensive) estate-bottled varietals, all 100% of the grape named. The Barbera and Zinfandel are aged five years in wood before bottling.

Edward and Phyllis Pedriezetti took over the winery in 1963 from his father, John. He had purchased it in 1945 from Camillo Colombano, who built it in 1923. The third generation is represented by young Daniel Pedrizetti.

In addition to the two reds mentioned above, the Pedrizettis offer estate-bottled Grenache Rosé and Zinfandel Rosé, as well as whites, aperitif and dessert, sparkling and fruit wines at their tasting room in the "Gallery" just north of Morgan Hill.

Richert & Sons, Inc., Morgan Hill

Walter S. Richert, a 1932 graduate of the University of California, is a remarkable man and there are many who say he is brilliant. He is certainly very modest by nature. He first entered the wine industry in 1937 and has been connected with wineries in various capacities as chemist, winemaker, production manager, sales representative and general manager. He has held important positions in the American Society of Enologists (winemakers) and has been Editor of both *Wine Review* and *Wines and Vines.*

In 1953 he founded his own winery at Morgan Hill on a shoestring, expanding gradually as opportunities permit. In 1958 he took over the old Paradise Valley Winery at Oak Glenn a few miles west of Morgan Hill.

A retail outlet is maintained in the front part of the Richert home facing Highway 101 at Morgan Hill right next door to the site of the former Madrone Winery now no longer in existence.

The winery's four-cask trademark represents Walter Richert and his three sons, Robert, Eric and Scott (daughter Barbara Jean was not included). All four children received their Social Security cards before they were eight, and have been associated with the winery, in Richert's words, "in either a positive or negative way since its founding." Eric is deceased. Robert entered the business full time after graduating from college in 1969, and Scott was to graduate from Fresno State with a degree in enology in 1972. "The two sons' ambition is to kick the old man out of the business," Richert said, "and mine is to have them do it fast."

Richert & Sons continues to specialize in four Sherries and two Ports, generally considered to be among the best in California. Recently the firm entered the fruit wine business, and Robert and Scott plan to start table wine production.

"The old man" promises to revive the *Richert Report,* a witty and informal journal of the winery's progress issued to clients and friends.

San Martin Vineyards Company, San Martin

In the heart of the Santa Clara Valley's vineyard land lies the well known San Martin Vineyards Company. This family enterprise is owned by the closely knit Filice family which originally came from the Province of Cosenza in Calabria, Italy and members of which are spread all over Central and Southern Europe. The Filice antecedents in the wine business are said to date back to around the year 1700.

A branch of the Filice family settled in California in the Santa Clara Valley in the early eighteen eighties and planted considerable land there in the early part of the century. In 1932 Bruno Filice, who also had wine interests in Italy, acquired the old San Martin Winery and Vineyards which had been founded forty years before. Since then a great many changes and improvements have been made in modernizing the winery and installing new equipment.

The family concern is owned and operated by Bruno Filice's children, grandchildren and in-laws. Peter Filice is president, Michael is vice president, John is secretary-treasurer and Frank is plant superintendent. Pasquale Lico is cellarmaster and the wine maker. Michael Filice Jr. is the vineyard manager and Michael Bo the chemist. Fred A. Lico is executive director and Bruno Filice is executive vice president.

Over a thousand acres of vineyards are under cultivation, most of which were planted by members of the family. They are situated on the sunny western hillside of the Santa Clara Valley, many of them on the slopes of Mount Madonna, dominating the Hecker Pass, and include Glen Loma and Castlewood, planted to the choicer varietal vines. A new 400-acre area is under development on the eastern Santa Clara Valley slope.

A magnificent new tasting room and retail outlet was recently opened right on Highway 101 near the handsome ivy-covered San Martin Winery. Others are in San Francisco, Monterey and San Jose. Visitors entering the tasting room find themselves in an atmosphere of wine use rather than production. If they wish they can go to the elaborate wine bar with its carved oak oval backdrop where host bartenders, versed in the use of wine, offer a 14-wine and champagne tasting program! Sales are not pushed but all the San Martin wines are attractively displayed should one wish to make a purchase.

A full line of table wines, sparkling wines, aperitif and dessert wines including vermouths and fruit wines are available, *San Martin* being the featured brand.

The *San Martin* bottle fermented sparkling wines include: *Brut* (very dry), *Extra Dry* (medium) and *Demi Sec* (fairly sweet) Champagne as well as Pink Champagne and Sparkling Burgundy. A specialty is the Spumante Moscato, a sparkling Muscat made by the traditional Italian method.

San Martin is the featured brand for the specially aged aperitif and dessert wines and for the Berry Wines made from fresh berries from the Santa Clara Valley: Strawberry Fraisette, Blackberry (Boysenberry Variety) and Loganberry.

Montonico, a tawny wine, on the sweet side, produced from the vines of that name imported from Calabria and whose advent was already announced in this *Guide* some years ago, is available now. Another specialty is Mokka Lau, a coffee flavored beverage.

Bertero Winery, Gilroy (Hecker Pass)

A winery in the western foothills of the Santa Clara Valley in the Hecker Pass area.

Alfonso Bertero, the founder, was born in the neighborhood of Turin in Italy and came to this country in 1911. He first worked for the Standard Oil Company and in 1919 went into the wine business, selling grapes to home wine makers and to other wineries for the production of sacramental wines. He moved to his present location in 1924, where he built the winery and his home. The property is part of the old Los Alamos grant and some of the original Spanish wooden stakes survive.

Bertero, who has since passed away, turned the family enterprise over before he died to his son Angelo, who in turn is aided by his sons, Angelo Jr. and Carl.

Table wines only are produced, all from local grapes. Burgundy is available as well as Sauterne (from the French Colombard grape). Varietals include Pinot Noir, Cabernet Sauvignon, Barbera, Zinfandel, Grignolino, Chardonnay and Semillon. Outstanding is the winery's Grenache Rosé, made exclusively from that grape. *Bertero* is the winery's main brand.

Bonesio Winery, Gilroy (Uvas district)

A winery well known in the surrounding counties, producing sound "country" Santa Clara table wines. It is located in the hilly Uvas district west of Gilroy near the Hecker Pass, *uvas* being Spanish for grapes and the region so named because the Spaniards, presumably, already raised or found grapes there. The property forms part of the former Solis Rancho, and the Bonesio residence, over a hundred years old, was once the headquarters of the large Solis Rancho grant.

Pietro (Peter) Bonesio, the founder of the winery, came from an Italian wine making family and was born in Cardona near Asti in Piedmont, Italy. He came to the United States in 1903 and worked in subway construction in New York City. He later farmed in Louisiana and then moved to Oakland, California, where he was engaged in the concrete business. In 1915 he reverted to the traditional family occupation, first starting a winery in the Rucker district, north of Gilroy. In 1921 Peter Bonesio bought the 600-acre Solis Rancho which has been the family home since.

Peter Bonesio lived until 1966, but turned the bsuiness over in 1932 to his sons Louis and Victor. The business is now owned and operated by Louis Bonesio who was brought up in the enterprise since his earliest days, being taught the trade by his father.

The Bonesio specialties include Grenache Rosé, Emerald Riesling, White Malvasia, Grignolino, Cabernet Sauvignon and Zinfandel.

The winery bottles under various labels, but the *Uvas* brand label is used for their finer wines.

SANTA CRUZ COUNTY

Bargetto's Santa Cruz Winery, Soquel

Founders of this family firm were the brothers Philip and John Bargetto, sons of Giuseppe Bargetto, wine grower and winemaker from the neighborhood of Asti in Piedmont, Italy. Giuseppe came to this country but then returned to his native land. His sons, however, both came over to stay. Philip came in 1887 and worked for some twelve years in the old Delmas Winery near San Jose. John immigrated in 1929 and first engaged in the produce and grape shipping business. In 1933 Philip and John founded the Bargetto Winery in Soquel which was owned by John Bargetto until his death in 1964. It is now owned by his son Lawrence, the winemaker, chemist and general manager. Two daughters of Philip complete the family membership of the enterprise.

The Bargetto wines are produced from grapes purchased from vineyards scattered over Santa Cruz and Santa Clara counties. Table wines are the specialty while aperitif and dessert wines, including a Marsala, round out the line.

Bargetto is the featured brand for premium wines. Besides the regular generic types the following varietals are generally available:

REDS: Barbera, Pinot Noir, Cabernet Sauvignon and Zinfandel;

WHITES: Chenin Blanc, Johannisberg Riesling, Sylvaner, Pinot Blanc and Vintage 1946 Moscato D'Oro (Golden Muscat);

ROSÉ: Grenache Rosé and Zinfandel Rosé.

All table and fruit wines are produced and bottled at the Bargetto Soquel winery.

Under the *Winemaster* brand generic wines are available for hotels and restaurants.

Nicasio Vineyards, Soquel

This winery owned and run by Dan Wheeler and a partner, Darlene Donovan, is located some six miles north of Soquel near Santa Cruz. After three years of home wine making Wheeler bonded Nicasio Vineyards in 1955.

Dan started wine making in the belief that fine wines should be 100% varietal, free of sulphur dioxide and stored at an even temperature the year around. To provide a perfect nest for his wines he started, back in 1952, to dig a cave into a sandstone hill down the road a little from his home. It is gradually being enlarged and is composed of two rooms devoted to storage and tasting purposes with an average temperature of 58 degrees F., varying but little throughout the year.

The winery may be small but the devotion inspiring it is as great as its wines are fine. Two hilltops have been cleared to make room for a small vineyard. Access to the upper vineyard is by a road that winds half a mile through a redwood forest.

A neighboring vineyard is planted to Johannisberg (White) Riesling, Chardonnay and Cabernet Sauvignon grapes. The Wheeler wines are made from these grapes and from Pinot noir obtained from hillside vineyards near Soquel. They also produce a Rosé made from Zinfandel and bottle fermented Champagne, with no dosage added at all, of the French *Nature* type, very dry but without harshness, made from the White Riesling, Chardonnay and Pinot Noir grapes, and produce and market a Chardonnay table wine.

Both Dan and his partner are hard workers. For Dan, a senior engineer of an electronic manufacturing company, the winery is also a retirement plan but far more than just a hobby. Darlene Donovan is an active real estate broker who has long been interested in fine wine.

The packaging of the Wheeler wines is elegant, in keeping with the contents. Besides the Champagne *Nature,* the following vintage table wines are available in small quantities from the winery and by mail order:

WHITE: Johannisberg Riesling, Chardonnay;
RED: Cabernet Sauvignon, Zinfandel;
ROSÉ: Zinfandel Rosé.

The Nicasio Vineyards wine labels are distinctive and individually signed. The brand reads: *Wine by Wheeler.*

F. *MONTEREY AND SAN LUIS OBISPO COUNTIES*

MONTEREY COUNTY

Chalone Vineyard, Soledad

This small winery, owned by a corporation founded in 1965 and reorganized in 1970, began making wines in 1966. They are of very high quality.

The property is the former F. W. Silvear Vineyard, the owner of which died in 1957. It passed through different hands until its purchase by Chalone Vineyard Ltd., headed by Richard H. Graff as president and winemaker, with Thomas L. Wilkerson as vice president. The first wines were Chardonnay, Chenin Blanc, Pinot Blanc and Pinot Noir.

Still wines are stored in small Limousin oak barrels in the manner of the classic French Burgundies, and all work is done by hand with reliance on volunteer labor supplied by the families and friends of the shareholders.

The land consists of 160 acres (about 100 planted to vines) on Stonewall Canyon Road about 10 miles from Soledad. The owners of Chalone Vineyard are happy to have visitors, but they ask that advance appointments be made by mail, since the winery is located seven miles from the nearest telephone or electricity!

San Luis Obispo County

Pesenti Winery, Templeton

A small, family operation founded in 1934 by Frank Pesenti, this winery nonetheless has won many awards at the Los Angeles County and California State Fairs for the quality of its products.

Frank Pesenti, now in partnership with his son, Victor, and son-in-law, Aldo Nerelli, still is active. *Pesenti* wines include the normal generics, as well as Cabernet, Zinfandel and Zinfandel Rosé. Notable among the whites is Chateau D'Oro, a light, sweet table wine, and Chateau Blanc, medium sweet. The wines of this company are sold only in the local area, where they have earned a just reputation, and from the winery tasting room off U. S. Highway 101.

York Mountain Winery, Templeton

Representative of good wine making in San Luis Obispo County is the York Winery, owned and operated by Max Goldman and located just below the peak of York Mountain on the eastern slopes of the Santa Lucia Mountains overlooking Templeton and the valley below.

The ranch property was acquired in 1882 by Andrew York. Born in Indiana Andrew came out West from Missouri in the eighteen fifties and settled in San Luis Obispo County after first having spent some time in the Napa Valley. A proud family possession is the original deed to the land, dated 1875, made out to Jacob B. Grandstaff from whom Andrew bought it, and signed by U. S. Grant, President of the United States.

Andrew York found that the grape vines he had planted to supplement his apple orchard yielded more grapes than he could market and so, with the help of his sons, Walter, Thomas and Silas, built a small winery to take care of the surplus. Shortly after the turn of the century additional land was purchased and a large vineyard planted of Zinfandels, selected because they mature early and thereby usually miss the early winter frosts. About that time too the winery was enlarged with the use of bricks molded and burned on the place in the ancient tradition of the Babylonians.

The York place is a historic one, as times goes, and many tales are told of how the lumber to build the original houses and winery was carted over the rough and steep mountain roads all the way from Cayucos on Estero Bay which at that time was a small flourishing harbor before the railroad came to Templeton. Indians used trails running through the property and camped overnight on the mountain on their way to the hot sulphur and mud baths in what is now Paso Robles, twelve miles distant. Nearby also is the San Ygnacio Ranch, established by Ignace Jan Paderewski, the great Polish patriot and world famous pianist, who raised wine grapes and had them crushed at the York Winery.

After the death of Andrew in 1913 his sons Walter and Silas took over the family enterprise which became the York Brothers Winery. Upon their retirement in 1944 the third generation wine makers, Wilfrid and Howard, continued the operation until 1954 from which time Wilfrid ran it in sole proprietorship until 1970.

The new owner, Max Goldman, bought the winery after 37 years as a winemaker, chemist and executive in California and New York. He will continue to produce the award-winning *York Mountain* Zinfandel, and will add a Champagne to be produced from new plantings of Chardonnay and Pinot Noir. He has also planted Cabernet Sauvignon, and has refurbished the building, adding a tasting room.

XII

THE GREAT INLAND VALLEY REGION

*C*HIS VAST VALLEY region sweeps down in a fairly narrow band parallel to the coast line, from which it is separated by the mountains of the Coast Range. Some three hundred miles long, it stretches from north of the city of Sacramento down south beyond Bakersfield in Kern County. Its climate, moderately warm in the northern areas, becomes progressively hotter the farther south one comes.

The region takes in the territory of both the Sacramento and the San Joaquin river valleys. It is the home of the great California aperitif and dessert wine production, for which the climate and soil are especially well suited. Most of the vines are cultivated by irrigation.

From north to south we have the *Lodi-Sacramento,* the *Escalon-Modesto,* and the *Fresno-San Joaquin Valley* districts.

A. *LODI—SACRAMENTO DISTRICT*

This district takes in the wine producing areas of Sacramento County and of the northern part of San Joaquin County.

In Sacramento County there is a wine growing area which stretches east of the city of Sacramento down southward, where both table and dessert wines are produced. Elk Grove is a center famous for its production of berry and fruit wines.

Northern San Joaquin County contains the famed wine growing district of Lodi, which spreads out to a surrounding region some ten miles deep. Lodi is on the Mokelumne River, which flows into the San Joaquin and is sometimes referred to as lying in the upper reaches of the San Joaquin Valley. It can also be said to be situated at the juncture of the Sacramento and San Joaquin valleys and in what is known as the Central Valley.

Lodi, recognized as a separate viticultural district, is especially noted for its aperitif and dessert wines. It is the center of a vast Flame Tokay vineyard district, spectacular in the fall due to the brilliant coloring of the grapes. The Flame Tokays are mainly used as table grapes, but are also employed in many of the dessert wines produced by the Lodi wineries including the wine called tokay.

Sacramento—Elk Grove District

Gibson Wine Company, Elk Grove

Robert H. Gibson, founder of the company, turned to the production of wines after first having been a successful stockbroker both in his home town of Cincinnati, Ohio, and in New York City.

He felt that many people would enjoy wines made from other fruit than grapes and experimented for some years in the production of berry and fruit wines. His faith was fully justified and he succeeded in developing a large market for his products. Berry and fruit wines have come into their own (see Chapter IX) and the Gibson Wine Company has become one of the largest producers in this field.

Robert Gibson, Bob as he was known to his friends, spent much of his time in Roseville, California, where he had a large cattle ranch and raised rare pheasants as a hobby. It is not surprising therefore that the trademark of the corporation is the *Golden Pheasant* which appears on many of its labels and is blown into most of its bottles. Bob Gibson died in 1960.

A large and modern bottling plant is maintained in Covington,

Kentucky, just across the Ohio River from Cincinnati, to which the company ships its wine in bulk from California to be bottled and marketed in the Middle West and the East.

The Elk Grove Gibson Winery, where most of the company's berry and fruit wines, as well as the table and aperitif and dessert wines are produced, was originally a gas engine works. In 1934 it was converted into a winery, Robert Gibson acquiring the property in 1943. From a small plant it grew into a modern and up to date winery, producing the best known berry and fruit wines in California.

Louis W. Schulze is now the firm's president and Jack Schulze is vice president in charge of western sales. Bud Jones is winemaker.

The *Gibson's Old Fashioned* brand is used for the berry and fruit wines.

Gibson's Premium Select is the featured brand for the usual table and aperitif and dessert wines. *Vinesse* is used for the Champagne and Cold Duck.

LODI DISTRICT
(Northern San Joaquin County)

Barengo Cellars, Acampo

The winery, the former Acampo Winery, is just north of Lodi. Dino Barengo, a graduate of the University of Nevada, is the owner, general manager and winemaker.

Barengo has been associated with the Acampo Winery since the early forties, when it was a stock corporation of which Cesare Mondavi, who later took over the Charles Krug Winery, was president. In 1943 the Acampo Winery was acquired by the Gibson Wine Company, now of Elk Grove, and Dino Barengo managed it for that concern. Barengo then leased the winery and finally purchased it in 1946, when he became the sole proprietor.

Both table and aperitif or dessert wines of sound standard quality are produced, with *Barengo, Barengo Reserve* and *Barengo Cellars* the featured brands.

Alex's Winery (Coloma Wine Cellars), Lodi

Founded in 1935 by a Greek, Christ Alexander, Alex's Winery products have become widely known through a system of company-owned retail outlets and tasting rooms. More noteworthy, however, is the acquisition in 1965 of Coloma Wine Cellars at the historic community of Coloma in the Mother Lode, the town where gold first was discovered in California.

A company operated by Alexander's sons, George and Dennis, and wine consultant Wallace H. Pohle, has undertaken to restore the winery and a portion of that was once a 3,700-acre wine growing area. Plantings of prime varietals will be tested with the hope of revitalizing one of California's principal former winery regions.

Alexander Cellars is the brand for standard quality generic wines and brandy and for Retsina and Kokineli, both Greek-type wines with the flavor of resin. In addition, the winery produces a rice-flavored *Mount Fuji* sake. The *Coloma Cellars* brand is reserved for premium wines, many of them made in the Napa Valley and bottled at Lodi. The varietals are as follows:

WHITE: Johannisberg Riesling, Riesling, Chardonnay, Green Hungarian and Chenin Blanc;

RED: Barbera, Cabernet Sauvignon, Gamay Beaujolais and Pinot Noir;

ROSÉ: Grenache Rosé.

Aperitif, dessert and sparkling wines are offered under both labels.

East-Side Winery, Lodi

This well known winery, one of the largest in the district, is a farmers' co-operative, founded in 1934. Its name was adopted because the area East of Lodi where the winery is located is known for its particularly rich soil yielding high quality grapes.

The co-operative is formed by 130 growing farmer-stockholders to whom all returns are made after costs and taxes have been paid. Ole R. Mettler is president of the co-op, Leon Kirschenmann vice president and Ernest C. Haas general manager.

The regular types of generic table and of aperitif and dessert wines are produced with *Royal Host* the featured brand. Brandy, under the same label, is an important specialty.

In 1962, after a great deal of study, East-Side entered the premium wine field, with well-aged aperitif wines and several varietals, including Chenin Blanc, Grey Riesling, Semillon, Emerald Riesling, Gold and Ruby Cabernet, the latter three made from new California grapes developed by the University of California at Davis.

Guild Wine Company, Lodi

Formerly known as the "Wine Growers Guild" the name was changed in 1959 to "Guild Wine Company" as this better describes the enterprise and its activities. It is a grower-owned co-operative of wineries composed in turn of about 1,000 individual growers. Guild is the third largest wine producer in the U.S.

Most of the wines are finished and bottled at Lodi, but are made at eight producing wineries from Ukiah in the north to Delano in the south. On March 1, 1971, Guild acquired the California wine brands and inventories of Schenley, including Roma at Fresno and the historic Cresta Blanca brand originally from Livermore, as well as the Schenley wineries at Fresno and Delano.

Alta Vineyards Co. was founded in 1949 as successor to the Alta Winery, Cameo Vineyards Co., A. Mattei and B. Cribari and Sons. Garrett & Co. involved two great complexes, the oldest dating back to 1935 when the Garrett family established its firm in Medoc, North Carolina, in the heart of the vineyard region of the South. By the time of the merger with Guild, Garrett & Co. owned 7,000 acres of vines and three wineries in California and additional acreage and wineries in North Carolina and the Finger Lakes District of upper New York. In 1945, the Garretts acquired the Guasti operation from the Italian Vineyard Co., founded in 1883 by Secundo Guasti, a native of Italy's Piedmont. At its height, I.V.C. had 5,000 acres of vineyards, and Guasti had established a town for his workers, complete with houses, a store, firehouse, school, church and an inn.

The driving force behind the development and expansion of the Garrett holdings was Captain Paul Garrett who, before his death in 1940, was a dominant figure in the American wine industry. The company was carried on by members of his family until the merger with Guild.

L. K. Marshall, one of the great men in the history of California wine, was president of Guild from its inception in 1943 until his retirement in 1957. He died soon after. Hubert Mettler is now chairman of the board. Guild's president is Robert M. Ivie, a Stanford graduate active in all phases of the wine industry who, as a hobby, experiments growing varietals at his home in Atherton. The vice president in charge of production is W. E. Kite and Lawrence Quaccia is quality control manager and chief winemaker.

The regular types of table wines and of aperitif and dessert wines including vermouth are marketed under the *Winemasters Guild* brand, the table wine for which the company is best known being the familiar "Vino da Tavola," a sweet red table wine of the Vino Rosso order, launched by the company as a new type of wine back in 1950.

The Lodi district has been recognized as a separate viticultural district and accordingly Guild Wine Company are marketing a Lodi Tawny Port and a Lodi Cream Sherry under their *Winemasters Guild* label. These are both distinctive wines and the appearance of the appellation of origin in the name seems a most welcome development. In this author's opinion the San Joaquin Valley's famed wine districts should receive infinitely greater recognition on the labeling than heretofore. The public and the trade should be made familiar with the fact that the San Joaquin Valley is—or should be —to the premium aperitif and dessert wines what the northern coastal counties are to the premium table wines and champagnes.

The Guild Wine Company also produces and markets Pale Dry Sherry, Cream Sherry and Tawny Port under the *Ceremony* "Old San Francisco Brand" label. These are Lodi district wines aged in small oak cooperage.

Ceremony is also used for (bulk fermented) Sparkling Wines (Champagne, Pink Champagne and Sparkling Burgundy) but the most celebrated products marketed under the *Ceremony* label are undoubtedly the company's straight dry Brandies, 5 and 8 years old, the latter being considered by many an expert to be one of the finest and smoothest brandies produced in California. The *Guild* "Blue Ribbon" Brandy is a blended and sweetened product similar in character to the majority of California brandies marketed. It should be noted that all the Guild Wine Company's brandies are produced from the Tokay grape for which the Lodi district is famous and which lends itself well for brandy distillation.

Other Guild Wine Co. brands used in various parts of the United States include:

Table and dessert wines: *Virginia Dare, Roma, Cresta Blanca, Garrett, Famiglia Cribari, Mendocino, J. Pierrot* and *La Boheme;* Sparkling wines: *Guild, Tres Grand, Cook's, Cribari, Jeanne D'Arc, Versailles, La Boheme, Cresta Blanca, Roma* and *J. Pierrot;* Brandy: *Roma, St. Mark* and *Citation.*

B. *ESCALON—MODESTO DISTRICT*

This district covers the wine growing areas and wineries of the southern part of San Joaquin County, from Stockton south and southeast to Manteca and Escalon; it takes in Stanislaus County from Salida on down to Modesto and also includes the Livingston area in northern Merced County.

The Escalon-Modesto district, located in the northern San Joaquin Valley, is best known for its dessert wines, but table and sparkling wines are also produced. Some of the California wineries with the largest distribution are located in this district.

Escalon District
(Southern San Joaquin County)

Franzia Brothers Winery, Ripon

This family corporation, located about halfway between the towns of Manteca and Escalon in the southernmost part of San Joaquin County, is owned and operated by the five Franzia brothers. They are the sons of the late Giuseppe Franzia (Joe Sr.), a native of Genoa, Italy, who immigrated to this country, settling first in San Francisco and then moving to Stockton. He purchased the Franzia ranch in Ripon in 1906 and was for many years prominent in the grape-shipping business and from 1933 until his death in 1952 in the wine producing field.

Giuseppe Franzia's sons carry on the family wine making tradition, Joseph being the president of the firm, John the secretary and treasurer, and Frank, Louis and Salvador vice presidents in charge of the various departments. Fernando Quaccia is the winemaker and chemist.

The Franzia policy is to produce and market sound standard quality wines at popular prices. The dessert wines are all produced exclusively from San Joaquin Valley grapes and so are the white table wines. The red table wines are blends of San Joaquin Valley and north coast counties wines, the latter mostly from the Napa Valley.

MODESTO DISTRICT
(Stanislaus County)

Pirrone Wine Cellars, Salida

This winery was founded by Frank Pirrone, an immigrant from Italy who became an architect in his adopted country. The vineyards were acquired in 1924 and the grapes sold to private individuals for home wine making. It was not until 1936 that the winery, designed by Frank Pirrone, was erected. The original capacity of 250,000 gallons has been expanded by more than a million, and a distillery has been added for the production of grape and peach brandy for addition to aperitif and dessert wines. A plant built in New Jersey to bottle wines for distribution in the East continued in operation until the early 1950's.

The present owners are Frank Pirrone's son, Alfred, and his wife,

Lois. He graduated in food technology from the University of California, where he studied under the late Prof. W. V. Cruess. With their three children, Kathy, Alfred and Ann, the Pirrones are assured of a third generation carrying on the family business.

Although Alfred Pirrone has started experimental plantings of new table wine varietals such as Ruby Cabernet and Royalty, all of the wine produced now is sold in bulk to other companies. He selects, ages and bottles premium varietals from other parts of California and makes them available from the winery's large and attractive tasting room. Expanded distribution is planned for the future.

E. & J. Gallo Winery, Modesto

The *Gallo* wines are familiar to a great many people and the success of this enterprise has been tremendous, good reasons to delve into the philosophy of the two brothers, Ernest and Julio Gallo, the owners. What is their thinking? What makes them tick? With the cooperation of the Gallo Brothers themselves, the reader will find out.

Now it is a fact that wine consumption in the United States is pitifully small (about a gallon per capita yearly) as compared particularly with France (43 gallons), Italy (34 gallons) or Spain (28 gallons).

Along with many others the Gallos studied this matter for years, trying to learn why Americans drink so little wine in comparison with some of those other countries, all the more surprising as the United States ranks among the larger wine growing countries of the world.

Ernest Gallo came to the conclusion that there are at least three reasons why consumption is so much greater in the foreign countries mentioned:

1. The wines of those countries are made more to the liking of

their peoples than are American wines made to the American taste;

2. Wines in foreign countries are priced to encourage their widespread use in volume;

3. Wine is displayed to suggest frequent use in volume.

Guided by these basic reasons the full resources of the Gallo research organization at the winery were—and are—devoted to the development of wines that will mean to Americans what Spanish wine means to the Spaniards, Italian wine means to the Italians and French wine means to the French. The idea being to develop a wine that was necessarily different from anything produced heretofore in this country or for that matter in any country, a wine tailored to the taste of millions of Americans who would buy wine in volume if they found one to their liking. A wine, also, that would be at a price level encouraging its use as an everyday refreshment beverage as well as being served with meals.

The Gallo Winery believes it has developed such a wine, a wine that has received the typically American name of "Ripple."

We are ahead of our story. . . .

It is certain that the Gallo brothers remain dedicated to their objective, undertaken when they founded their winery in 1933, to provide American homes with good, sound wines at popular prices. They attribute their progress towards that goal to the company's continuous scientific research for new, modern ways to improve the efficiency of grape growing and of wine making and to enhance the taste appeal of wines for American consumers.

One of the keys to Gallo's growth is the company's view that because wines are perishable, the only way to establish wine as a staple beverage in the American diet is to make certain (or as certain as humanly possible) that the consumer will be fully satisfied with every bottle purchased. This is why Gallo wines are bottled only at the winery where they are made and sealed under supervision of the company's own expert enologists in Gallo's exclusive "Flavor-Guard" bottles.

This bottle is the reason why the Gallo family in 1958, at a cost of more than six million dollars, built their own glass factory adjoining the Gallo Winery at Modesto. The glass, it is stated, protects the wine from the effects of ultra violet light rays. Gallo, it is believed, is the only winery in the world to manufacture its own bottles.

Gallo's research begins with the grapes. In the Gallo vineyards in Stanislaus and Merced Counties a large number of grape varieties are grown which the company constantly tests for its blends of wine while Gallo's viticulturists also guide other growers in producing grapes for the company.

Gallo's wines are made from grapes grown in the viticultural districts where they thrive best. In addition to the original Gallo winery at Modesto there are Gallo Cellars at Fresno and Cucamonga and eight grower owned wineries in Napa and Sonoma Counties producing wine for the company under the latter's supervision.

Convinced by many years of research that glass-lined steel tanks are preferable, Gallo has adopted that method of cooperage, using what are virtually giant bottles.

Modesto, the home of Gallo wines, is in the heart of the historic County of Stanislaus with its wine growing tradition dating back to about 1854 when George H. Krause, a native of Germany, laid out what was to become his famed Red Mountain Vineyard on part of the old Mexican grant El Rancheria del Rio Stanislaus.

It was in Modesto in 1933, the last year of Prohibition, that the Gallo brothers visualized the coming rebirth of the California wine industry, dormant during the dry years. They thought of creating a modern winery and planned that some day homes throughout the nation would proudly serve wines from shiny bottles bearing their name.

It was an ambitious plan for the brothers. Ernest was twenty-four and Julio a year younger. They had been brought up in the tradition of good wine, born as they were in the third generation of a wine growing family whose forebears had cultivated vineyards and made wine in Italy's famed Province of Piedmont. The Gallo brothers had been educated in the public schools of Modesto and knew about viticulture firsthand, having worked in the family's vineyards. They borrowed and scraped together enough dollars to rent a warehouse in Modesto to house a few casks and a grape crusher to serve as a winery until they could build one of their own. In that old warehouse the first Gallo vintage was crushed and fermented that same year, 1933, a historic one in the Gallo story.

A few months later they built a small wine cellar on the outskirts of Modesto. This first concrete structure on the banks of Dry Creek was carefully planned as the first unit of the winery the Gallo brothers envisioned. It was built and ready for use in 1935.

At first the Gallos made only red table wines, selling them in bulk to wholesale bottlers. In 1937 they were able to build an extension to their cellar and to install further equipment. They began to produce port, sherry and muscatel in addition to their table wines. They studied modern developments in viticulture and wine making and searched for the best types of cooperage and other winery equipment. Julio Gallo devoted himself increasingly to the development of the most suitable grape varieties in the family's vineyards and to the production of wines while Ernest Gallo studied consumer and trade problems and marketing.

In the Gallo vineyards at Modesto, which the family had owned since 1925, new varieties were grafted onto old rootstocks. Additional vines were planted to grow the choicer varieties suited to local and climatic conditions. Gradually the Gallos increased their vineyard acreage, planting vines in the Keyes district of Stanislaus County and acquiring a vineyard near Livingston in Merced County.

The Gallo brothers realized that Fresno and the Southern San Joaquin Valley region yielded grape varieties most desirable for the sweeter dessert wines while Napa and Sonoma in the Northern Coastal Counties provided the best grapes for dry table wines. Accordingly they selected grapes from these districts to complete their assortment of wines.

It was not until 1940 that the Gallos felt they were producing wines of the quality they wanted to market in bottles bearing the family label. It was in that year, another milestone in the Gallo saga, when their wines first appeared on the market. A following of consumers soon developed and Gallo advertising began.

From a small beginning in California and Louisiana the *Gallo* wines gained a steady and increasing acceptance. The company concentrated on trying to please the consumer. The Gallo brothers and their staff interviewed buyers of their wines to learn the exact characteristics of wine flavor, of dryness or sweetness and of color that would please householders. They talked to retailers and salesmen to learn what their customers wanted and they strove to get their wines efficiently displayed and stocked. Year after year they were introduced in additional markets from coast to coast and their sales continued to grow.

There is no doubt that the Gallos have contributed and are contributing much to making wine ever more popular as a national beverage in the United States.

By 1970 Gallo was marketing more than forty types of wine, all bottled at their Modesto winery. Over thirty were of the traditional types, led by the most popular generic table wines, the usual types of aperitif and dessert wine including vermouths and berry wines, Boone's Farm Apple Wine and Concord Grape. In addition there are Vin Rosé, "Paisano" the popular wine of the Vino Rosso order, and "Pink Chablis," one of their most successful.

In 1966 the Gallos introduced *"The Vintners of Eden Roc"* line of bulk fermented champagnes. The following year the name was adopted for a brandy, and in January of 1968, *Old Decanter* brand Livingston Cream Sherry was added, named for the Livingston vineyard in Merced County. The company has continued to expand to the point where its capacity is more than 100 million gallons, including contract affiliates. A new $1.5 million headquarters building has been erected at Modesto.

In 1957 Gallo launched its flavored aperitif wine "Thunderbird" which rapidly became very popular. In 1959 "Gypsy Rose," a pink aperitif, was introduced.

Here we see clearly the Gallo philosophy at work, that of introducing altogether new wines, specifically suited, it is hoped, to the American taste and thereby capturing a large market of their own. So far, they have been remarkably successful and there can be no doubt that the Gallos are smart merchandisers.

Here we are back to the beginning of our story and the "Ripple" Wines, both Red and White, launched by Gallo in 1960. They are quite special and pleasing in their way, with an ever so slight effervescence placing them in the "Table Wines Plus" class (see Chapter V).

No doubt more new wines will be produced and launched by the energetic Gallos seeking to please the American palate. One great advantage of having successful proprietary names is to have consumers guided back to one's products, the aim being not only to produce new wines but also to create a captive market.

What is the author's reaction to all of this? It is quite simple. He believes that there will always be a market for the traditional types of wine, for which California has become famous, notably for the varietals. He believes that there is also room for new types of wine, such as Gallo and other wineries have launched. If they are successful, all the more power to the launchers and to those who created them.

After all, Dubonnet did not always exist in France, and neither did a number of other French aperitifs. There is nothing wrong with them and neither is there with "Thunderbird" or "Gypsy Rose" if people like them. And as far as slogans are concerned is there any difference, in principle, between "Du Beau, Du Bon, Dubonnet" and "Everyone Goes for Gypsy Rose"?

So let us welcome all and sundry newcomers in the wine field. Only time will tell whether or not they will occupy a permanent place in the American home.

C. *THE MOTHER LODE*

The Mother Lode is the name traditionally applied to the historic Gold Rush country of the Sierra foothills, stretching 250 miles from Mariposa east of Merced, north to Downieville in Sierra County. It has never been regarded as one of California's classic wine-growing regions, but some wineries, such as the previously mentioned Coloma Wine Cellars, are well over a century old. These are a few representative samples.

TUOLUMNE COUNTY

Butler Winery, Sonora

Completed in 1970 after three years of construction, this winery was founded by J. L. Butler with his two sons, Roger and Marcus, as winemaker and sales manager respectively. Although it has a Sonora mailing address, the winery actually is located in the quiet forest behind Twain Harte, near Cedar Ridge. The younger Butlers purchased their father's interest and now operate as partners.

They make only red table wines, including two rosés, from grapes harvested in specially selected vineyards. Their best so far seems to be the Zinfandel which, like all Butler wines, is naturally clarified without filtration. The storage capacity is only 10,000 gallons, all in small oak casks.

Also produced is a unique fruit wine from the wild elderberries that grow in the foothills.

Columbia Cellars, Columbia

Founded the same year as the Butler Winery, Columbia Cellars also is a family operation. H. Spencer Hoffman is the owner-wine-maker, assisted by his wife when it comes to bottling, labeling and waiting on customers. Fermenting is carried out in redwood tanks, and aging and storage in small oak cooperage. A normal line of dry table wines is available, as well as a number of unique dessert wines, including Spice Jubilee and Columbian Gold.

The large, A-frame winery on Parrots Ferry Road is open to the public seven days a week all year, and is the only place *Columbia Cellars* wines may be purchased. An extensive display of old mining equipment works in with the motif of the community as a restored Gold Rush boomtown.

AMADOR COUNTY

D'Agostini Winery, Plymouth

Since 1911, the year the D'Agostinis took over the vineyards laid out by a Swiss immigrant named Adam Uhlinger in 1856, a cadre of loyal consumers has been trekking to the old stone winery northeast of Plymouth to buy hearty red wines.

In often harsh weather, the 125 acres of hillside vines surrounded by dense woods are tended by Armenio D'Agostini and his family, Tulio, Michele and Henry.

Several improvements and additions have been made since the time Uhlinger sold wine to the prospectors, and the winery is solidly prosperous. *D'Agostini* Burgundy and Zinfandel are the most popular.

EL DORADO COUNTY

Gold Hill Winery, Coloma

Another new winery, this one was founded by John and Beverly Hempt in 1969. Their seven-acre vineyard, a vestige of those days a century ago when the neighborhood boasted 3,700 acres of grape vines, is planted to Chenin blanc, Johannisberg Riesling and Cabernet Sauvignon. Aging wines are stored in small barrels of European and American oak.

A winemaker and vineyardist, Hempt was born in Europe and educated in Yugoslavia, Hungary, Germany and the United States. In addition to limited quantities of estate-bottled table wines (some of which won't be available for some time) the winery offers fruit and berry wines at its tasting room and gift shop in historic Coloma, the site of John Marshall's discovery of gold in 1848. Brands are *Gold Hill, Village Wines* and *Chateau René.*

D. *FRESNO—SAN JOAQUIN VALLEY DISTRICT*

This great district coincides with the lower San Joaquin Valley. It is famous especially for yielding wines of the sweeter dessert types, some of which have achieved great excellence. Table wines and bulk fermented sparkling wines are also produced.

The district takes in the following counties, from north to south: Madera, with the city of Madera the main sector;

Fresno, with its many famed wineries located in the city of Fresno and in the surrounding towns, with other famous wineries to be found in Sanger, Reedley, Parlier, Fowler, Selma and Kingsburg;

Kings, with its Hanford area;

Tulare, with the main winery centers in Dinuba, Cutler, Tulare, Lindsay, and on the Kern County line right across from Delano;

Kern, with Delano and the sector east of Bakersfield down to Arvin the wine production areas.

A number of well known wineries located in this district do not produce wines directly for the public under their own brands and are, for that reason only, not discussed in this *Guide*.

Madera District

Bisceglia Brothers Wine Co., Madera

This enterprise was founded in 1888 by four Bisceglia brothers, Joseph, Pasquale, Bruno and Alphonse, who came from a family of vineyardists and winemakers in Cosenza, Province of Calabria, Italy. They first settled in California in the Santa Clara Valley where they went into the wine business and also operated a large cannery. In 1939 the canning operation was discontinued and they directed their full attention to the wine business.

The large and modern winery the Bisceglias are now operating was completed in 1947 and has a capacity of nearly eight million gallons. Standard quality table, sparkling and aperitif and dessert wines are produced and distributed throughout the country.

The last of the original founders, Alphonse F. Bisceglia, passed on in 1952 and the family members now running the enterprise are Bruno T. Bisceglia, president, and Joseph A. Bisceglia, vice president.

Paradise is the leading brand while *Golden Chalice,* introduced in 1953 after years of research, is used for wines of a character all their own, the dessert wines being very sweet.

Ficklin Vineyards, Madera

A small and unique operation, the only California winery specializing in port and the first winery in the United States that made port wines produced entirely from choice Portuguese grape varieties commercially available. The Ficklin Ports rate as the finest produced in California, being unsurpassed in quality and character with a full richness of flavor.

The Ficklin wine concern, founded in the middle of the nineteen forties, has made quite a name for itself and deservedly so. It is a family enterprise, the principal owners and operators being David (Dave) B. Ficklin, the winemaker and a well known wine judge, and his brother Walter C. Ficklin Jr., the vineyardist.

Their father, Walter C. Ficklin Sr., a charming gentleman familiar with all the better things of life, first came to California as a young man in 1911, making his home in Fresno County and planting his first vineyards and orchards in 1912. For many years he farmed grape and fruit ranches. In the early forties the family became interested in the idea of producing red dessert wines of top quality. They closely studied the Portuguese wine grape varieties which were being tested by the University of California under local growing conditions. The decision to establish a completely specialized vineyard complex and winery was the next step. Five of the finest Portuguese varieties were selected, Tinta Cão, Tinta Madeira, Alvarelhão, Souzao and Touriga, and the vineyards planted to them exclusively. A small but modern adobe winery was built by hand and 1948 saw the first vintage harvested.

The greatest care is taken to produce the very best wines possible. The vineyards are meticulously tended to yield a limited crop of the choicest grapes. At harvest time the grape clusters are individually cut with small hand shears and all imperfect fruit is left on the vines. They are first lightly crushed in stainless steel crushers, breaking the skins and separating them from the stems. The crushed grapes are transferred to small open vats where pure yeast culture is added. As soon as fermentation starts a wooden hand plunger is used to submerge and mix the skins with the juice, extracting thereby the full color and flavor of the grapes. The free-run juice is drawn off and the skins are given a further light pressing in a basket-type press, the resulting juice being added to the free-run for further flavor. At the proper stage of fermentation the juice is transformed into port wine by the addition of pure grape brandy. The wine is clarified naturally by gradual settling and racking in small oak puncheons or barrels. It is aged in oak for three years or longer and at least a further year in the bottle. Owing to this process, the Ficklin Ports, like those from Portugal, will throw a slight sediment, a sign of maturing and of age. The wines, therefore, should be poured carefully, so as not to disturb the deposit, or be decanted before serving. If disturbed, the bottle should be placed upright until the wine has had a chance to settle.

The main variety of Port available is the Tinta Port, a blend of the varieties grown. It is a full Ruby and is marketed under the *Ficklin Vineyards* brand.

A feature of the Ficklin operation is the use of a special pot still beverage brandy for the spirits addition. This gives the finished product considerable additional character, the wines possessing a harmonious bouquet and flavor when mature.

In addition there is a program of Special Bottlings of Vintage Ports, available only in small quantities direct from the winery. Several vintages of Tinta Maderia have been earmarked for this special program, good news for the numerous Ficklin *aficionados*.

The Ficklins have experimental plantings of Emerald Riesling and Ruby Cabernet, grape varieties developed by the University of California. Table wines have been produced on a pilot scale program, and only are available at the winery from time to time. The emphasis remains on producing what has been described by some experts as Ports among the finest in the world.

Fresno District
(Fresno County)

Nicholas G. Verry, Inc., Parlier

Located at Parlier some eighteen miles southeast of Fresno this winery is mainly devoted to the production of Retsina, the resin flavored wine which is especially popular with those of Greek origin.

The founder and president of the company, Nicholas Verry, was born in Sparta, Greece, in 1896. He came to this country when he was a boy of ten but has often returned to Europe on visits and business trips. He learned the art of wine making from his brother-in-law, George Solomos, a well known enologist and chemist of Sparta.

Nicholas Verry is assisted in the family enterprise by his wife who bears the noble name of Athena and is secretary-treasurer of the company while their son, John N. Verry, is vice president.

The Verry family first established themselves in the wine business in California in 1933 with a winery in Glendale, moving to their present location in 1942.

Besides Retsina the winery also produces a wine called *Philery* (Quick Love), a light wine, produced in the same manner as Retsina but without the resin flavoring and possessing its own distinctive bouquet and flavor.

TULARE COUNTY

California Growers Wineries, Cutler

This co-operative winery was organized on April 20th 1936 and began operations at their present address on July first of the same year. It is owned and operated by 18 growers who have been in the grape industry for many years.

From the beginning, the grower-members have required the personnel at the winery to produce quality wines and grape brandy. Part of the philosophy of California Growers Wineries is that the farming interest of the growers, so important a part of the California and national agricultural picture, should be harmoniously balanced with those of the producer and the merchandiser of California wines.

The officers of California Growers Wineries are the following: Robert Setrakian, president; Leonard P. Le Blanc, vice president; Floyd Olsen, secretary-treasurer; Richard Lequia, assistant secretary-treasurer. Nino Muzio is the winemaker.

California Growers Wineries specialize in the production of sherries, sweet wines of the "dessert" type and grape brandy, the featured brands being *Growers Old Reserve* and *Growers*.

XIII

SOUTHERN CALIFORNIA REGION

*T*HIS, THE THIRD of the great wine producing regions of California, covers the southern part of the state, from Los Angeles and San Bernardino counties down south to the Mexican border. Its over-all climate is warm, though less hot than that of the San Joaquin Valley in the great inland valley region. It is especially noted for its dessert wines, while good table wines, notably of the red varieties, and champagnes of quality are also produced.

Southern California consists of a number of separate wine producing districts of which the Cucamonga district in the southwestern tip of San Bernardino County is the best known. It is followed by the city and county of Los Angeles.

There are two further districts in the region, the Riverside district in the northwest section of Riverside County adjoining Cucamonga and the Escondido district centering around the city of that name in San Diego County. No wineries of more than local importance are located in the last two districts, although some very good dessert wines are produced there, notably muscatels in the Escondido district, where the Muscat of Alexandria grape attains its highest quality. It was in San Diego County that the Franciscan missionary Padre Junipero Serra planted, according to tradition, the first Mission vines in 1769.

A. *CUCAMONGA DISTRICT*

Cucamonga, one of the few places in California to retain its old Indian name, is said to be derived from "Cucamongabit," meaning "Land of Many Springs." Cucamonga Indians were living in the district when the Spaniards came and built their El Camino Real. In 1839 Don Tiburcio Tapia, who became president of the Ayuntamiento, or City Council, of Los Angeles and the city's first *alcalde,* obtained the Cucamonga grant from the Mexican Government. It is known that Don Tapia also planted grape vines on the ranch.

Cucamonga was the scene of many turbulent events in its early days and its history makes fascinating reading. Gradually it passed from the violent and romantic Wild West stages to an equally romantic but more peaceful era of agriculture and industry. Magnificently situated in the San Bernardino Valley in the extreme southwestern corner of the county of that name, it lies at the foot of the grandiose range of the San Gabriel Mountains with Cucamonga Peak dominating the scene from an altitude of some 8000 feet.

The Cucamonga wine growing district has become increasingly famous over the years. It centers around the town of Cucamonga, straddling Highways 66 and 99 and spreading north to Etiwanda and Alta Loma and south to Ontario, Guasti, and the Riverside County line. It is threatened, however, like many other wine growing areas, by the encroachment of real estate developments.

The Cucamonga district is noted for its red table wines, especially Barbera, Grignolino, Zinfandel, and Chianti. These should be consumed young, as they mature early, owing to the warm climate in which the grapes are grown. New plantings of white varieties such as Emerald Riesling and even Chardonnay have been undertaken. Cucamonga is also well known for its champagnes and aperitif and dessert wines, including ports, sherries, and vermouths.

Cucamonga Vineyard Company, Cucamonga

The enterprise, formerly the Padre Vineyard Company, is now known as the Cucamonga Vineyard Company. The winery, founded in 1870, was rebuilt by the Vai family in 1909 and enjoys the distinction of being California's Bonded Winery No. 1. Mrs. James L. Vai, widow of a legendary figure in the California wine industry who contributed much to making Southern California's wines famous, is president, while Cesare Vai is vice president. Marvin Osburn Jr. is secretary-treasurer and Primo Scorsatto is the winemaker, and chemist.

At present the firm concentrates on custom bottling of table wines, aperitif and dessert wines including vermouths, champagnes and other sparkling wines, and brandy. The production personnel is highly experienced and as highly regarded. The premises, situated in the heart of the Cucamonga District, contain the bonded winery No. 1, a fruit distillery, a rectifying plant and a bonded warehouse.

The featured house brand is now *San Gabriel,* formerly marketed by the famed old San Gabriel Winery, no longer in existence. *Sic tempus fugit.*

Cucamonga Winery, Cucamonga

This winery claims to be the original one of the district with the Cucamonga name and has contributed a great deal to make the Cucamonga names famous for its table wines, not only in California but also in the Eastern part of the country. It is mainly owned and operated by the Accomazzo family.

Alfred (Fred) Accomazzo and his brother Eduardo, natives of San Desiderio in the Asti region of Piedmont, Italy, came to Southern California as young men in 1902. Alfred soon engaged in the wine and liquor business and then established his first Bonded Winery in Glendale, California, in 1916. During Prohibition he turned to the real estate business but with Repeal again became identified with the wine industry, this time permanently.

The Cucamonga Winery was founded in 1933 when Alfred Accomazzo joined forces with several partners to operate a winery in the heart of Cucamonga. Vineyards were acquired and soon extended. With careful attention to the arts of wine growing and wine making the firm produced high quality wines which, when introduced to the Eastern markets, gained immediate recognition and have maintained a growing reputation wherever they have been marketed.

The Accomazzo family owns the majority of the stock in the Cucamonga Winery enterprise. Alfred Accomazzo passed away in 1960 but his son, Arthur, and Edmund E. (Ed), a son of Eduardo Accomazzo, continued the family tradition while Sam Kurland is also prominent in the firm.

It is interesting to note that some of the Cucamonga Winery's vineyards, running to 850 acres, are irrigated and others are not. While the North Coast Counties' vineyards are non-irrigated and those in the Great Inland Valley Region mostly are, those in Southern California are often mixed. This *Guide* has refrained from indicating whether particular vineyards are irrigated or not in areas where either might be the case because, as the Accomazzos point out, the idea that non-irrigated vineyards produce better grapes in warm climates is not always correct. In extremely dry years or in a succession of dry years non-irrigated vineyards will produce crops of grapes lacking the necessary qualities to make good wines. On the other hand, irrigated vineyards should never be over-irrigated. The answer is the *proper* amount of water, whether vineyards are irrigated or not and that is the responsibility of a good vineyardist or wine grower.

The Cucamonga Winery produces only red and white table wines (and Vermouth) one of the few in the district to do so. All are of premium quality, the reds being more typical of the district. They are mainly distributed in the East and Midwest. The featured brand is *Romano Cucamonga,* the slogan "Wines to Remember."

The regular types of generic table wines are available as well as

Chianti, and Dry Muscat and the following red varietals: Barbera, Grignolino and Zinfandel. *Alfredo* is the brand for Vermouth.

Assumption Abbey Winery

(see **Brookside Vineyard Company,** below)

Brookside Vineyard Company, Guasti

The owners of this historic family enterprise are the Bianes, wine growers and wine makers in the district for five generations. Philo Biane, the president of the firm, has been in the wine business of the region continuously for over sixty years.

The firm was originally founded by Théophile Vaché who came from his native island of Oléron in France by way of Cape Horn to California in 1830. Two years later he is said to have engaged in the wine business in Monterey, then still under the Mexican flag. He certainly was one of the pioneers of the California wine industry as in 1849 or even earlier he planted vines south of Hollister in San Benito County in the so-called "Vineyard District" later to become the Valliant Vineyards, now leased by Almadén (see there).

Three nephews of Théophile Vaché the elder came to California to join their uncle: Émile, Théophile the younger and Adolphe. A fourth brother, Alfred, remained in France to operate the family winery and distillery. Émile later returned to his native country as did Théophile the elder but Théophile the younger and Adolphe remained in California. Eventually the family moved to Southern California founding a wholesale business of fine wines and spirits in the heart of downtown Los Angeles. In 1882 the Vaché brothers established themselves as "Wholesale Dealers and Rectifiers and Manufacturers of Native Wines, Brandies, Wine Vinegar, Syrups, Etc.," at Old San Bernardino, leasing the winery which Dr. Benjamin Barton had built some years before. The next year they moved to Redlands Junction, hardly a town at that time, some ten miles southeast of San Bernardino, where they built the Brookside Winery.

A French lad by the name of Marius Biane arrived in 1892 from his native district of Gers in Gascony and soon went to work for the brothers Vaché at Brookside. He fell in love with Marcelline, Adolphe Vaché's daughter, and married her. In due course the Biane family carried on the Vaché tradition of wine making in Redlands, Marius also acquiring vineyards in the Cucamonga district. In 1916 the winery was sold and Marius Biane's sons, Philo and François, went to work for Garrett & Company and later for Fruit Industries Ltd., as the California Wine Association (see there) was known at one time. It was not till 1952 that the Bianes revived their own enterprise by re-establishing the Brookside Vineyard Company at Ontario, moving in 1956 to Guasti at their present location.

The Guasti plant which the Bianes purchased from the California Wine Association, built in 1904, has vast storage cellars with walls of stone, three feet thick. One of the units has an underground space, 20 feet below the surface, 175 feet long by 100 feet wide, used for the storage and aging of wines prior to shipment.

Marius Biane has since died. His son, Philo, is president and general manager. The fifth generation of the wine making family is represented by Philo's sons, Michael and Pierre, and by René, the son of François (Frank) Biane who passed away in 1958.

The featured brand for premium wines is *Brookside* and under this label generic table wines and Zinfandel as well as aperitif and dessert wines including dry and sweet vermouth are available. *E. Vaché* is a subsidiary brand.

The Brookside Winery has for long been noted for its Altar Wines and in its expansion and promotion of the finer wines was approached by the Benedictine Monks of Assumption Abbey, Richardton, North Dakota, to enter into working arrangements with them whereby it would be possible to start the Benedictines in the wine business in the New World, following their ancient Old World tradition.

This was accomplished and so the Assumption Abbey Winery was formed as a D.B.A.* of Brookside Vineyards Company and the *Assumption Abbey* brand was launched.

The Benedictine Monks, one of the oldest orders of the Roman

* Doing Business As.

Catholic Church, have been characterized by lives devoted to prayer, study and labor. Though devotion is primary, they exemplify Saint Benedict's Rule that monks "live by the work of their hands." Their 1400 year background in the production of wines and related beverages is known the world over. The wonder and skill of the Benedictines' art in wine making and to uplift the heart of man is now captured in Assumption Abbey wines, carrying on the world respected and centuries old Benedictine tradition.

Abbot Hunkler, who was the Abbot of Assumption Abbey when the project began, was known throughout the Benedictine communities as the "Wine Abbot." He has been replaced by Abbot Robert West, and the Abbey's wines, produced by the Bianes at their Brookside Winery in Guasti, enjoy a national distribution, from New York to California and from Louisiana to Minnesota.

The wines sold to the public include Cabernet, Dido Noir and Zinfandel in the reds; St. Emilion and Vertdoux Blanc in the whites, and Vin Rosé. Aperitif and dessert wines are Tinta Port, Sherry Palido, Sherry De Oro, Sherry Crema, Cream Marsala and Cream Muscat.

Assumption Abbey Altar wines are available to the clergy under the same brand. In addition to the still wines mentioned above, there are two bottle-fermented champagnes, *Brut* and Extra Dry, and an aged brandy.

In 1969 Brookside acquired the 12 Mills Winery roadside cellars in Northern California, making the company, with 16 cellars of its own already in the south, the largest direct-to-the-consumer winery operation in the country.

Brookside also has started new vineyards in the Rancho California agricultural complex at Temecula, an area designated by University of California scientists as Regions II and III, similar to the Napa and Sonoma valleys. The company has 1,000 acres under its control, and plans call for 5,000 acres eventually. The first varietals from the new vines, Petite Sirah, Emerald Riesling and Johannisberg Riesling, were on the market in 1971.

B. *THE CITY AND COUNTY OF LOS ANGELES*

Where some ten years ago Los Angeles still counted twelve wineries, this number has now decreased to a few wineries and bonded cellars. No more, alas, is the old San Gabriel Winery in operation at San Gabriel. The time when Los Angeles led California in wine growing and wine production has long since passed. Real estate developments, freeways and other changes of the times, such is the price one has to pay for progress. Often willingly, let it be said. Where Anaheim once was a German colony devoted to the growing of wines, it is now the home of Disneyland.

The first new winery to be established in Los Angeles since 1917 was founded in 1970 by Les Navé, a rocket test engineer from Hollywood, and Sam Pierson, a former professional photographer, of South Pasadena.

The modest Navé Pierson Winery and tasting room in the city's industrial area offers a dozen sound to excellent red and white table wines and fruit wines.

"We are, right now, small vintners with large ambitions," the partners said. "Our chief goal, when you really get down to it, is to disagree, by virtue of our products, with the popular belief that fine wine must come from a bottle with both dust and a high price on it."

With a final tribute to the memory of Jean Louis Vignes and his famed Aliso Vineyard that once covered over a hundred acres of what is now the heart of downtown Los Angeles and with a bow to the Mission Fathers headed by Fra Junipero Serra who were the first to plant and cultivate grapes along the shores of the Pacific, Part Two of this *Guide* comes to a somewhat reluctant close.

Part Three

XIV

HANDY WINE AND FOOD GUIDE

*W*HAT WINE to serve with a particular dish or at a special occasion? At what temperature will a wine taste the best and give the most value for the money? This and related information is presented chartwise in the following pages.

The how and when of serving wines has been overdone. It has also been underdone. Wines *are* at their best at certain temperatures. Certain wines *do* go better with certain foods. There is no point in denying the facts. After all, coffee tastes better hot than tepid and orange juice is tastiest when cold. The same with wines. Red table wines will give the greatest enjoyment when served at the temperature of the room and white table wines when they are chilled. Lukewarm champagne is to no one's liking and overicing it will kill its natural flavor and bouquet. Stirring champagne with a swizzle stick is idiotic, killing the very bubbles it has cost a fortune and centuries of experience to create. So it is really only sage to observe certain very simple rules.

Suggestions follow for nearly every occasion. Should you not agree with them, you can always suit yourself.

A. *WINE WITH, BEFORE AND AFTER MEALS*

Eleven O'Clock (Elevenses)

with English biscuits or cookies....Sherry (dry or medium), *Brut* or *Extra Dry* Champagne

Lunch

before lunch.....................Sherry (dry or medium), *Brut* Champagne

with lunch.....................Grenache Rosé, Gamay Rosé or other Rosé; *White table wine:* Semillon (dry or medium), Sauvignon Blanc (dry or medium), Chardonnay, Pinot Blanc, Chenin Blanc, Folle Blanche, White (Johannisberg) Riesling, Traminer, Sylvaner, Grey Riesling

with picnic lunch................Grenache Rosé, Gamay Rosé or other Rosé

Afternoon Refreshments

with cookies or cake.............Port, Muscat, Sherry (medium or sweet); *Extra dry* or *Demi Sec* Champagne; Grenache Rosé, Gamay Rosé or other Rosé

Cocktail Party (6–8 o'clock)

with canapes....................*Brut* or *Extra Dry* Champagne, Sherry (dry, medium or sweet), Port, Muscat, Sweet Vermouth

Cocktail Party (6–10 o'clock or later)

with ham, turkey, cold cuts or
casserole dinner................*Brut* or *Extra Dry* Champagne;
Cabernet Sauvignon, Pinot Noir or
Gamay; Grenache Rosé, Gamay Rosé
or other Rosé

Dinner

before dinner....................*Brut* or *Extra Dry* Champagne; Dry
Sherry or Dry Port

with dinner (one wine, white or
red, depending on the main
course, see B. Specific Dishes)..RED: Cabernet Sauvignon, Pinot
Noir, Gamay, Zinfandel, Barbera,
Grignolino
WHITE: Semillon (dry or medium),
Sauvignon Blanc (dry or medium),
Chardonnay, Pinot Blanc, Pinot
Blanc de Noir, Chenin Blanc, White
(Johannisberg) Riesling, Traminer
or Gewurztraminer, Sylvaner, Grey
Riesling

with dinner (one wine regardless
of dish).......................*Extra Dry* Champagne throughout
with formal dinner (two entrees)...If white and red, first the white, then
the red; if two reds, Cabernet Sau-
vignon followed by Pinot Noir

with dinner (one table wine and
one with the dessert)...........Red or white table wine with the
main course
With the dessert: Sweet Semillon,
Sweet Sauvignon Blanc, Chateau
Sauterne, *Demi Sec* or *Sec* Cham-

pagne, Moscato Amabile, Moscato Spumante, Port, Muscat

after dinner......................Brandy

Supper (after the theatre)

regardless ....*Brut* or *Extra Dry* Champagne

Nightcap

with a snack.....................A split (¼ bottle) of *Extra Dry* or *Demi Sec* Champagne, Port, Muscat, Sweet Sherry

At Any Time of Day or Night

with English biscuits or cookies....*Brut* or *Extra Dry* Champagne

B. *WINE WITH SPECIFIC DISHES*

THE DISH   THE SUGGESTIONS

Before the Meal

Canapes or Hors d'Oeuvres........*Brut* or *Extra Dry* Champagne, Dry Sherry

Caviar or Lumpfish..............*Brut* Champagne

Oysters, Fish and Shellfish

Oysters or Clams.................Chardonnay, Pinot Blanc, White (Johannisberg) Riesling, Traminer, Sylvaner, Grey Riesling; *Brut* or *Extra Dry* Champagne

Fish or Shellfish, plain (boiled, broiled, poached).............Semillon (dry or medium), Sauvi-

gnon Blanc (dry or medium), Chardonnay, Pinot Blanc, Chenin Blanc
(dry), Folle Blanche, White (Johannisberg) Riesling, Traminer, Sylvaner, Grey Riesling, Green Hungarian

Fish or Shellfish, creamed.........Semillon (medium or sweet), Sauvignon Blanc (medium or sweet),
Chenin Blanc (sweet)

Soups

Clear Soup.....................Dry Sherry
Creamed Soup...................Medium Dry Sherry

Eggs and Salads

Eggs of any kind.................No wine as eggs and wine don't mix
Salads ....No wine as it does not blend with
vinegar or lemon

White Meat

Veal, Pork.....................Semillon (medium), Sauvignon
Blanc (medium), Chenin Blanc
(medium); Gamay, Zinfandel;
Grenache Rosé, Gamay Rosé or other
Rosé

Red Meat

Tournedos, Chateaubriand, Filet
  Mignon, Steak, Roast Beef......Cabernet Sauvignon
Pot Roast, Stew, Spareribs, Short
  Ribs, Meat Patties.............Gamay, Zinfandel
Beef Burgundy...................Pinot Noir
Steak and Kidney Pie............Cabernet Sauvignon, Zinfandel

Beef Stroganoff..................Gamay, Zinfandel
Lamb..........................Zinfandel, Gamay

Ham

Hot or Cold....................Semillon (medium), Sauvignon
                               Blanc (medium), Pinot Blanc, Pinot
                               Blanc de Noir; Grenache Rosé,
                               Gamay Rosé or other Rosé

Poultry

Chicken (broiled, roasted, fried,
    stewed)......................Red or white table wine.
                               RED: Cabernet Sauvignon, Zinfandel,
                               Gamay, Pinot Noir. For *white* table
                               wine choice see Fish or Shellfish,
                               plain
Chicken, creamed...............White table wine; for choice see Fish
                               or Shellfish, creamed
Turkey, roasted.................Red or white table wine, red pre-
                               ferred, see Chicken, broiled
                               On festive occasions: *Extra Dry*
                               Champagne or Sparkling Burgundy
Long Island Duckling, Goose......Cabernet Sauvignon, Gamay, Zin-
                               fandel, Pinot Noir

Game

Wild Duck, Partridge, Pheasant,
    Quail, Squab, Venison..........Cabernet Sauvignon, Gamay, Pinot
                               Noir

Rabbit

Tame or Wild...................Cabernet Sauvignon, Gamay, Zin-
                               fandel, Pinot Noir

Variety Meats and Frogs' Legs

Sweetbreads, Brains, Frogs' Legs...Semillon (medium or sweet), Sauvignon Blanc (medium or sweet), Chenin Blanc (medium or sweet), Traminer or Gewurztraminer

Kidneys, Heart, Tripe, Liver......Zinfandel, Gamay

Cold Cuts

At lunch, dinner or supper........Grenache Rosé, Gamay Rosé or other Rosé; Semillon (dry), Sauvignon Blanc (dry); Chardonnay, Pinot Blanc, Chenin Blanc (dry), Folle Blanche; White (Johannisberg) Riesling, Traminer, Sylvaner, Grey Riesling, Green Hungarian; Zinfandel, Gamay

Casseroles

Any of these.....................Red or white table wine depending on what the casserole is made of

Foreign and Exotic Dishes

Spaghetti, Macaroni, Pizza and
other Italian Dishes (Pastas)....Barbera, Grignolino, Charbono, Chianti

Goulash ....Zinfandel
Mexican Dishes.................Lager, Ale or Beer
Curried Dishes.................Lager, Ale or Beer
Indonesian Rijsttafel.............Lager, Ale or Beer
Highly Seasoned Dishes..........Lager, Ale or Beer

Cheese

Assorted Cheeses.................Cabernet Sauvignon, Pinot Noir, Port
Welsh Rarebit...................Lager, Ale or Beer

Dessert

Desserts, Fruit and Nuts..........Semillon (sweet), Sauvignon Blanc (sweet), Chateau (type) Sauternes, Chenin Blanc (sweet), *Demi Sec* or *Sec* Champagne, Moscato Amabile, Moscato Spumante, Port, Muscat.

C. *SPECIAL OCCASIONS*

Wedding Receptions.............*Brut* or *Extra Dry* Champagne
Christening Receptions...........*Brut* or *Extra Dry* Champagne
Birthdays and other anniversaries,
    men ....*Brut* Champagne
Birthdays and other anniversaries,
    women ....*Extra Dry* Champagne, Pink Champagne (Rosé)
New Year's Eve.................*Extra Dry* Champagne
As a gift for any occasion.........A bottle or case of any fine wine
Thanksgiving or Christmas Dinner.Cabernet Sauvignon, Pinot Noir, *Extra Dry* Champagne, Sparkling Burgundy or Champagne Rouge.

D. *GENERAL SUGGESTIONS*

Storage of Wines

The best place...................Cellar or closet
The temperature................About fifty-five degrees

The position.....................Lying down to keep the cork moist

The manner.....................Bins or shelves or wooden cases or cartons stood on edge; diamond shaped bins are the best but simple cartons with dividers will do very nicely.

Serving of Wines

White table wines................Cold, as they taste better that way, the sweeter the wine, the colder, but they lose their flavor when over-iced. Two to four hours in the refrigerator is about right.

Red table wines..................At the temperature of the room

Sparkling wines..................Cold, but not too cold. Two to four hours in the refrigerator is about right.

Rosé table wines................Same as white table wines (see above)

Sherry, Port, Muscat.............Same as red table wines (see above)

Should the bottle be opened before serving? ....Yes, to let the wine "breathe" and release its bouquet; open white wines one half hour, red wines an hour before serving

When should a wine be decanted?...In the case of fine table wines and Port wines that have thrown a deposit

What is the best wine to use in cooking?.....................The best and finest only, as they have the most character and flavor; in the case of table wines use the same wine for cooking as served at table with the dish

Who is served first?..............The host always, who pours a small amount in his glass to make certain the wine tastes right

Serving white California table
wine:.........................Semillon or Sauvignon Blanc; Chardonnay, Pinot Blanc, Pinot Blanc de
Noir, Chenin Blanc, Folle Blanche;
White (Johannisberg) Riesling, Traminer or Gewurztraminer, Sylvaner,
Grey Riesling

Serving red California table wines:..Cabernet Sauvignon, Zinfandel;
Pinot Noir, Gamay; Barbera, Gri-
gnolino, Charbono

Serving rosé California table wines:.Grenache Rosé, Gamay Rosé, Cabernet Rosé, Zinfandel Rosé, Grignolino
Rosé

Serving California Champagne:....*Brut* before the meal, *Extra Dry* during and *Demi Sec* or *Sec* with the
dessert; Pink Champagne for the
ladies

Serving California Sherry:.........*flor* or non-*flor Sherry,* but made
from the Palomino grape

Serving California Port:...........Tinta (Madeira) Port preferably

Serving California Muscat:........Muscat Frontignan (white) or Black
Muscat (red).

Note: Preference has been given here, as elsewhere in this *Guide,* to
the *varietal* wines as in general they will have the most character, bouquet
and flavor. They are also, both as far as character and as name are concerned, typically and distinctively Californian.

XV

MODERN WINE GLASSES

*T*HERE WAS A TIME, not long ago, when decent American wine glasses were hard to obtain. Americans, so generous in most other instances and inclined to like everything big and large and vast, clung for some unexplained reason to puny wine glasses that could do honor to no wine, let alone the host or hostess. They still cling to them, especially in the restaurants where a proper, generous sized wine glass is a rare thing to behold. Recently, thank goodness, American glass manufacturers have seen the light and fair sized wine glasses are available for the home to those who want them.

Modern usage, led by the French firm of Baccarat, the leader in wine glass ware for some centuries, demands wine glasses that are simple, pleasing, elegant in design and that hold about *twice as much wine as one is likely to serve in them.* They should be clear, easy to hold and without gingerbread.

In general the tulip or bowl shaped glasses are considered the most satisfactory. Their stems should be thin, but not too thin; they should above all hold enough to allow the wine to breathe and to release its bouquet. They should never be hollow stemmed as this makes it difficult to clean them adequately. They should be things of joy to own, to look at with pleasure. They should grace the table and shine or sparkle. They should never be small or puny.

A number of acceptable designs for wine glasses will be found on the following pages. They are suggestions only, adaptable to variations.

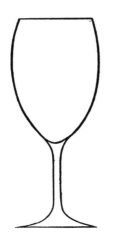

1. All purpose table wine
8 ounces

2. Claret or Burgundy
10 ounces

3. White wine
6 ounces

4. Rhine wine
5 ounces

1. All purpose table wine glass

Tulip shaped wine glass suited for any table wine, red, white or rosé, holding 8 ounces. A good all purpose type wine glass so that, owning no other wine glass, one still can be correctly prepared for any occasion.

2. Claret or Burgundy glass

Large tulip shaped wine glass, specially suited for a fine Cabernet Sauvignon or Pinot Noir or for any fine Claret or Red Burgundy. It holds 10 ounces but 12 ounces is also appropriate.

3. White table wine glass

Bowl or tangerine shaped wine glass designed for California white wines such as Semillon and Sauvignon Blanc; Chardonnay, Pinot Blanc, Pinot Blanc de Noir, Chenin Blanc or for any wine of the Sauternes, Graves, Chablis and White Burgundy families. It holds 6 ounces and can also be used at a dessert wine glass of Sweet Semillon, Sweet Sauvignon Blanc or Sweet Sauternes.

4. Rhine wine glass

Tall, curved bowl shaped wine glass specifically suited for any white wine of the rhine wine order such as White or Johannisberg Riesling, Traminer or Gewurztraminer, Sylvaner and Grey Riesling or for any wine, of course, of the Rhine and Moselle families. Contents 6 ounces.

Formerly such rhine wine glasses were green, amber or even rose in color; modern practice requires them to be crystal white.

5. Tulip Champagne glass

Tall tulip shaped champagne glass, holding 10 ounces and conforming to modern good taste. It is an elegant type glass, which has supplanted both the flute shaped champagne glass and the familiar saucer shaped champagne glass that is still to be found in many homes and in most restaurants and nightclubs.

5. *Tulip Champagne*
10 ounces

6. *Port or Muscat*
4–5 ounces

7. *Sherry or Aperitif*
4–5 ounces

The saucer champagne glass will be with us for years to come as it has become so strongly identified with the serving of champagne or any other sparkling wine. Yet the tall tulip shaped champagne glass is much more elegant, distinctive and better suited for the purpose. It should, of course, never be hollow stemmed (see introduction to this chapter).

6. Port or Muscat glass

This is a typical modern and pleasing dessert wine glass, suited well for Port, Muscat or for any other dessert wine, served either with the dessert or between meals with light refreshments. It holds 4 to 5 ounces and, like any other wine glass, should be about half filled.

7. Sherry or Aperitif glass

Contrary to popular belief, the best Sherry glasses are not the traditional V-shaped vessels which look as if they should hold Martinis, although they are the ones most often sold. Preferable are "chimney" glasses holding 4–6 ounces, capable of capturing and accentuating the aroma and bouquet of the wine.

XVI

A LIST OF OUTSTANDING
CALIFORNIA WINES

*T*HIS LIST is arranged according to wine type and alphabetically within the district where the wine is produced. Preference has been given to the varietal wines as being more typically Californian both in character and name. Vintage wines are indicated with (V).

While there may possibly be California wines as good as those listed here the author is certain that there are none better.

Awards received at the yearly State Fair at Sacramento and Los Angeles Fair are helpful but inconclusive to form an overall picture as not all wineries send their wines in to be judged and some never do.

In each category of this selective list certain wines will be finer than others. Every one is entitled to an opinion but one would have to be a combination of King Solomon and of a Supreme Court of Wines to make an exact, graduated classification as to their relative excellence. A solution is to try them all and to decide for oneself.

A. CALIFORNIA RED TABLE WINES

Cabernet Sauvignon (The premier claret type wine of California)
SONOMA COUNTY, Sonoma Valley
    Buena Vista Cabernet Sauvignon
MENDOCINO COUNTY
    Fetzer Vineyards

NAPA COUNTY, Napa Valley
  Beaulieu (B V) Georges de Latour Cabernet Sauvignon Private
                                                      Reserve (V)
  Heitz Cellar Cabernet Sauvignon (V)
  Inglenook Cabernet Sauvignon, Older Vintages and Special
                                                      Casks (V)
  Charles Krug Cabernet Sauvignon (V)
  Louis Martini Cabernet Sauvignon (V)
  Louis Martini Cabernet Sauvignon Special Reserve (V)
  Mayacamas Cabernet Sauvignon
ALAMEDA COUNTY, Livermore Valley
  Concannon Cabernet Sauvignon (V)
ALAMEDA COUNTY, Mission San Jose
  Llords & Elwood Cabernet Sauvignon
ALAMEDA COUNTY, Northern Alameda County
  Davis Bynum Private Reserve Cabernet Sauvignon
SANTA CLARA COUNTY, Santa Clara Valley
  Almadén Cabernet Sauvignon
  Gemello Cabernet Sauvignon
  Paul Masson Cabernet Sauvignon
  Martin Ray Cabernet Sauvignon (V)
  Ridge Vineyards Cabernet Sauvignon (V)
SANTA CRUZ COUNTY
  Nicasio Vineyards Cabernet Sauvignon (V)

Zinfandel (typical California red table wine of better than average qual-
  ity, fruity and zestful)
SONOMA COUNTY, Sonoma Valley
  Buena Vista Zinfandel
SONOMA COUNTY, Russian River Valley
  Pedroncelli Zinfandel
MENDOCINO COUNTY
  Parducci Zinfandel
NAPA COUNTY, Napa Valley
  Charles Krug Zinfandel
  Louis Martini Mountain Zinfandel (V)
  Souverain Cellars Zinfandel
SOLANO COUNTY

Cadenasso Zinfandel
ALAMEDA COUNTY
Bynum Zinfandel
CONTRA COSTA COUNTY
Viano Private Stock Zinfandel
SANTA CLARA COUNTY, Santa Clara Valley
Mirassou Zinfandel
Ridge Vineyards
SAN LUIS OBISPO COUNTY
York Mountain Zinfandel
SAN BERNARDINO COUNTY, Cucamonga District
Assumption Abbey Zinfandel
Cucamonga Winery Zinfandel

Pinot Noir (the great red burgundy type wine)
SONOMA COUNTY, Sonoma Valley
Buena Vista Pinot Noir
Hanzell Pinot Noir (V)
NAPA COUNTY, Napa Valley
Beaulieu (B V) Beaumont Pinot Noir (V)
Heitz Cellar Pinot Noir (V)
Inglenook Pinot Noir (V)
Louis Martini Mountain Pinot Noir (V)
ALAMEDA COUNTY, Mission San Jose District
Weibel Pinot Noir
ALAMEDA COUNTY, Northern Alameda County
Davis Bynum Private Reserve Pinot Noir (V)
SANTA CLARA COUNTY, Santa Clara Valley
Almadén Pinot Noir
Paul Masson Pinot Noir
Martin Ray Pinot Noir (V)

Gamay (the Beaujolais type wine)
ALAMEDA COUNTY, Livermore Valley
Wente Bros. Gamay Beaujolais
NAPA COUNTY, Napa Valley
Inglenook Gamay (V)
Charles Krug Gamay (V)

SANTA CLARA COUNTY, Santa Clara Valley
 Paul Masson Gamay Beaujolais
 Mirassou Gamay Beaujolais

Barbera (full flavored Italian type wine)
SONOMA COUNTY, Sonoma Valley
 Sebastiani Barbera
NAPA COUNTY, Napa Valley
 Heitz Cellar Barbera
 Louis Martini Mountain Barbera (V)
SAN BERNARDINO COUNTY, Cucamonga District
 Cucamonga Winery Barbera

Grignolino (light colored red wine of Italian origin, see also Grignolino
 Rosé)
NAPA COUNTY, Napa Valley
 Heitz Cellar Grignolino
SOLANO COUNTY, Suisun District
 Cadenasso Grignolino
SAN BERNARDINO COUNTY, Cucamonga District
 Cucamonga Winery Grignolino

Charbono (Soft Italian type red table wine of Piedmontese origin)
NAPA COUNTY, Napa Valley
 Inglenook Charbono (V)

Petite Sirah (the grape of France's Rhône Valley)
ALAMEDA COUNTY, Livermore Valley
 Concannon Petite Sirah

B. CALIFORNIA WHITE TABLE WINES

Sauvignon Blanc (the more aromatic of the Sauternes type wines)
ALAMEDA COUNTY, Livermore Valley
 Concannon Sauvignon Blanc (V)
 Wente Bros. Sauvignon Blanc (V)
NAPA COUNTY, Napa Valley

    Beaulieu (B V) Chateau Beaulieu
    Charles Krug Sweet Sauvignon Blanc
    Robert Mondavi Sauvignon Blanc
SANTA CLARA COUNTY, Santa Clara Valley
    Novitiate of Los Gatos Chateau Novitiate

Semillon (fruity and flavorful wine of the Sauternes type)
ALAMEDA COUNTY, Livermore Valley
    Concannon Dry Semillon
    Wente Bros. Dry Semillon
NAPA COUNTY, Napa Valley
    Beaulieu (B V) Dry Sauternes (principally Semillon)
    Charles Krug Sweet Semillon
    Louis Martini Mountain Dry Semillon (V)
SANTA CLARA COUNTY, Santa Clara Valley
    Almadén Dry Semillon
    Paul Masson Chateau Masson (Sweet Semillon)

Chardonnay (the Chablis and White Burgundy type wine)
SONOMA COUNTY, Sonoma Valley
    Hanzell Chardonnay (V)
ALAMEDA COUNTY, Livermore Valley
    Wente Bros. Pinot Chardonnay (V)
NAPA COUNTY, Napa Valley
    Beaulieu (B V) Beaufort Pinot Chardonnay (V)
    Heitz Cellar Chardonnay
    Martini Mountain Pinot Chardonnay (V)
    Mayacamas Pinot Chardonnay
    Stony Hill Chardonnay (V)
SANTA CLARA COUNTY, Santa Clara Valley
    Almadén Pinot Chardonnay
    Martin Ray Chardonnay (V)
    Mirassou Chardonnay
SANTA CRUZ COUNTY
    Nicasio Vineyards Chardonnay (V)

Pinot Blanc (White Burgundy type wine from the Pinot blanc grape)
ALAMEDA COUNTY, Livermore Valley
    Wente Bros. Pinot Blanc (V)

NAPA COUNTY, Napa Valley
  Heitz Cellar Pinot Blanc
SANTA CLARA COUNTY, Santa Clara Valley
  Almadén Pinot Blanc
  Novitiate of Los Gatos Pinot Blanc

Chenin Blanc (Vouvray type wine from Chenin Blanc or Pineau de la
  Loire grapes)
NAPA COUNTY, Napa Valley
  Inglenook White Pinot (V)
  Charles Krug Chenin Blanc
  Louis Martini Mountain Dry Chenin Blanc (V)
  Mayacamas Chenin Blanc (V)
  Robert Mondavi Fumé Blanc
  Souverain Cellars White Pinot
Folle Blanche (from that grape, a fresh, light luncheon wine)
NAPA COUNTY, Napa Valley
  Louis Martini Folle Blanche (V)

White Riesling or *Johannisberg Riesling* (the premier California wine
  of the Rhine wine order)
NAPA COUNTY, Napa Valley
  Beaulieu (B V) Beauclair Johannisberg Riesling (V)
  Heitz Cellar Johannisberg Riesling (V)
  Louis Martini Mountain Johannisberg Riesling (V)
  Souverain Cellars Johannisberger Riesling
ALAMEDA COUNTY, Livermore Valley
  Concannon White Riesling
SANTA CLARA COUNTY, Santa Clara Valley
  Almadén Johannisberg Riesling
  Mirassou White Riesling
SANTA CRUZ COUNTY
  Wines by Wheeler (Nicasio Vineyards) Johannisberg Riesling (V)

Traminer and *Gewurztraminer* (aromatic wine of the Alsatian type from
  the Traminer grape)
SONOMA COUNTY, Sonoma Valley
  Buena Vista Traminer (V)

NAPA COUNTY, Napa Valley
    Inglenook Traminer (V)
    Charles Krug Gewurztraminer
    Louis Martini Mountain Gewurztraminer
SANTA CLARA COUNTY, Santa Clara Valley
    Almadén Traminer

Sylvaner (light wine from Franken Riesling grapes)
SONOMA COUNTY, Sonoma Valley
    Buena Vista Sylvaner (V)
NAPA COUNTY, Napa Valley
    Louis Martini Mountain Sylvaner (V)
ALAMEDA COUNTY, Northern Alameda County
    Davis Bynum Franken Riesling
SANTA CLARA COUNTY, Santa Clara Valley
    Almadén Sylvaner
    Mirassou Sylvaner

Grey Riesling (light wine from Grey Riesling or Chauché gris grapes)
NAPA COUNTY, Napa Valley
    Charles Krug Grey Riesling
ALAMEDA COUNTY, Livermore Valley
    Wente Bros. Grey Riesling
ALAMEDA COUNTY, Mission San Jose District
    Weibel Grey Riesling
SANTA CLARA COUNTY, Santa Clara Valley
    Almadén Grey Riesling

Malvasia Bianca (light sweet wine from the grape of that name)
SANTA CLARA COUNTY, Santa Clara Valley
    San Martin Malvasia Bianca

C. CALIFORNIA ROSÉ TABLE WINES

Grenache Rosé (from Grenache grapes)
NAPA COUNTY, Napa Valley

Beaulieu (B V) Grenache Rosé
ALAMEDA COUNTY, Mission San Jose District
Weibel Grenache Rosé
SANTA CLARA COUNTY, Santa Clara Valley
Almadén Grenache Rosé

Gamay Rosé (from Gamay grapes)
NAPA COUNTY, Napa Valley
Charles Krug Vin Rosé
Louis Martini Mountain Gamay Rosé
ALAMEDA COUNTY, Livermore Valley
Wente Bros. Vin Rosé

Cabernet Rosé (from Cabernet Sauvignon grapes)
SONOMA COUNTY, Sonoma Valley
Buena Vista Rose Brook
NAPA COUNTY, Napa Valley
Beaulieu (B V) Beaurosé (from Cabernet Sauvignon, Gamay and
Mondeuse grapes)
ALAMEDA COUNTY, Mission San Jose
Llords & Elwood Rosé of Cabernet
ALAMEDA COUNTY, Northern Alameda County
Davis Bynum Cabernet Rosé

Zinfandel Rosé (from Zinfandel grapes)
SONOMA COUNTY, Russian River Valley
Pedroncelli Zinfandel Rosé
NAPA COUNTY, Napa Valley
Mayacamas Vineyards Zinfandel Rosé
Nichelini Vin Rosé
ALAMEDA COUNTY, Livermore Valley
Concannon Zinfandel Rosé

Grignolino Rosé (see also under Grignolino)
NAPA COUNTY, Napa Valley
Heitz Cellar Grignolino Rosé

D. CALIFORNIA CHAMPAGNE

Champagne
SONOMA COUNTY, Russian River Valley
    Korbel *Nature, Brut* and *Extra Dry*
SONOMA COUNTY, Sonoma Valley
    Buena Vista Pinot Chardonnay Champagne
NAPA COUNTY, Napa Valley
    Beaulieu (B V) Private Reserve Champagne *Brut, Brut* and *Extra Dry*
    Hanns Kornell Third Generation *Sehr Trocken, Brut,* Extra Dry and *Sec*
    Schramsberg *Blanc de Blancs* and *Blanc de Noir*
ALAMEDA COUNTY, Livermore Valley
    Concannon *Brut* and *Extra Dry*
ALAMEDA COUNTY, Mission San Jose District
    Weibel Chardonnay *Brut*
    Llords & Elwood Champagne
SANTA CLARA COUNTY, Santa Clara Valley
    Almadén *Blanc de Blancs* and *Brut*
    Paul Masson *Brut* and *Extra Dry*
    Martin Ray Madame Pinot Champagne (V, Blanc de Noir, from Pinot noir grapes) and Champagne de Chardonnay (V)
    Mirassou Champagne *Au Natural*

Pink (Rosé) Champagne
SONOMA COUNTY, Russian River Valley
    Korbel Rosé Champagne
NAPA COUNTY, Napa Valley
    Beaulieu (B V) Rosé Champagne (from Pinot noir grapes)
    Hanns Kornell Third Generation Pink Champagne (Rosé)
    Schramsberg *Cuvée de Gamay*
SANTA CLARA COUNTY, Santa Clara Valley
    Almadén Rosé (Pink) Champagne
    Paul Masson Pink Champagne
    Martin Ray Sang de Pinot (V) (from first light press of Pinot noir grapes)

Red Champagne (Sparkling Burgundy)
    SONOMA COUNTY, Russian River Valley
        Korbel Rouge Champagne
    NAPA COUNTY, Napa Valley
        Beaulieu (B V) Rouge Champagne
        Hanns Kornell Third Generation Sparkling Burgundy
    ALAMEDA COUNTY, Mission San Jose District
        Weibel Sparkling Burgundy
    SANTA CLARA COUNTY, Santa Clara Valley
        Almadén Sparkling Burgundy
        Paul Masson Sparkling Burgundy (Cuvée Rouge)

Moscato Amabile (slightly effervescent Muscat)
    NAPA COUNTY, Napa Valley
        Louis Martini Moscato Amabile

E. CALIFORNIA APERITIF and DESSERT WINES

Sherry (Dry, Medium and Sweet)
    SONOMA COUNTY, Sonoma Valley
        Buena Vista Ultra Dry Sherry
    NAPA COUNTY, Napa Valley
        Beaulieu (B V) Cream Sherry
        Louis Martini Pale Dry Sherry
        Souverain Cellars Los Amigos Sherry Sack (dry)
    ALAMEDA COUNTY, Mission San Jose District
        Weibel Solera *flor* Sherries
        Llords & Elwood "Great Day," "Dry Wit" and "Judge's Secret"
        Sherries
    SANTA CLARA COUNTY, Santa Clara Valley
        Almadén Solera Cocktail, Golden and Cream Sherries
        Richert & Sons Pale Dry and Triple Cream Sherries
    SAN JOAQUIN COUNTY, Lodi District
        Guild Pale Dry and Cream Sherries

Port (Ruby, Tawny and Vintage)
    SONOMA COUNTY, Sonoma Valley
        Buena Vista Vintage Port

NAPA COUNTY, Napa Valley
Louis Martini Tawny Port
ALAMEDA COUNTY, Mission San Jose District
Weibel "Governor's Rare" Port (from Tinta Madeira and other grapes)
Llords & Elwood "Ancient Proverb" Port
SANTA CLARA COUNTY, Santa Clara Valley
Almadén Solera Ruby and Tawny Ports
Novitiate of Los Gatos Port
Richert & Sons Tinta Madeira Port
SAN JOAQUIN COUNTY, Lodi District
Guild Tawny Port
MADERA COUNTY
Ficklin Tinta Port and Special Bottlings of Vintage Ports

Muscat de Frontignan
ALAMEDA COUNTY, Livermore Valley
Concannon Muscat de Frontignan
SANTA CLARA COUNTY, Santa Clara Valley
Novitiate of Los Gatos Muscat Frontignan

Black Muscat
ALAMEDA COUNTY, Mission San Joe District
Weibel Cream of Black Muscat
SANTA CLARA COUNTY, Santa Clara Valley
Novitiate of Los Gatos Black Muscat

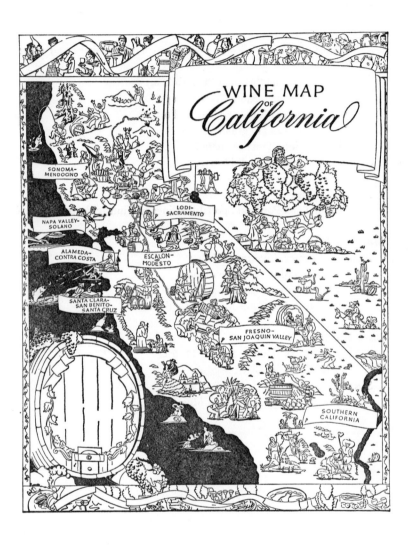

WINE MAP OF *California*

XVII

A LIST OF CALIFORNIA WINERIES
OPEN TO THE PUBLIC

Alameda County

ALBANY
> Bynum Winery
> 614 San Pablo Avenue
> 526-1366

LIVERMORE
> Concannon Vineyard
> P. O. Box 432
> HIlltop 7-3760
>
> Wente Bros.
> 5565 Tesla Road
> HIlltop 7-3603

MISSION SAN JOSE
> Weibel Champagne Vineyards
> P. O. Box 3095
> OLiver 6-2340

PLEASANTON
> Villa Armando Winery
> 124 St. Johns Street
> VIctor 6-5488

Alameda County (contd.)

PLEASANTON (contd.)
Ruby Hill Vineyard Co.
1188 Vineyard Avenue
846-2004

Amador County

PLYMOUTH
D'Agostini Winery
Box 66, Aukum Road
CHapel 5-6612

Contra Costa County

MARTINEZ
J. E. Digardi
P. O. Box 88
ACademy 8-2638

Conrad Viano Winery
Morello Road
228-6465

El Dorado County

COLOMA
Coloma Wine Cellars
P. O. Box 270
622-2275

Gold Hill Winery
P. O. Box 267
622-1712

Fresno County

FRESNO
Del Rey Cooperative Winery Association
5427 E. Central Avenue
AMherst 4-3441

Antonio Nonini Winery
2640 N. Dickenson Avenue
AMherst 4-7857

Fresno County (contd.)

FRESNO (contd.)
Roma Wine Company
3223 E. Church Avenue
AMherst 4-9671

KINGSBURG
Roma Wine Company
Sierra Street
TWinoaks 7-2984

PARLIER
Nicholas G. Verry Inc.
400 First Street
646-2785

SANGER
Sanger Winery Association
1720 Academy Avenue
TRinity 5-2505

Kern County

DELANO
A. Perelli-Minetti & Sons
P. O. Box 818
725-3501

EDISON
Giumarra Vineyards Corporation
P. O. Box 98
366-7251

Los Angeles County

LOS ANGELES
Nave Pierson Winery
1204 San Fernando Rd.
221-0167

Los Angeles County (cont'd.)

Los Angeles (contd.)
    San Antonio Winery, Inc.
    737 Lamar Street
    223-1401

San Gabriel
    Viotti Winery
    8606 E. Elm Avenue
    ATlantic 6-7474

Whittier
    Old Mill Winery
    1955 So. Workman Mill Road
    OXford 5-0305

Madera County

Madera
    Bisceglia Bros. Wine Company
    25427 Avenue 13
    673-3594

    Ficklin Vineyards*
    30246 Avenue 7½
    674-4598

Mendocino County

Redwood Valley
    Fetzer Vineyards
    Rt. 1, Box 361X
    485-8671

Ukiah
    Parducci Wine Cellars
    Route 2, Box 572
    HOmestead 2-3828

* By appointment only.

Napa County

CALISTOGA
  Schramsberg Vineyards*
  WHitehall 2-4558

NAPA
  Mayacamas Vineyards
  1155 Lokoya Road
  BAldwin 4-4030

  Mont La Salle Vineyards
  P. O. Box 420
  BAldwin 6-5566

OAKVILLE
  Oakville Vineyards
  P. O. Box 87
  944-2455

  Robert Mondavi Winery
  P. O. Box 403
  963-7156

RUTHERFORD
  Beaulieu Vineyard
  WOodward 3-3214

  Inglenook Vineyard Company
  WOodward 3-2116

ST. HELENA
  Beringer Bros.
  2000 Main Street
  WOodward 3-2725

  Chappellet Winery*
  1581 Sage Road

* By appointment only.

Napa County (contd.)

ST. HELENA (contd.)
Freemark Abbey
WOodward 3-7106

Heitz Wine Cellars
436 St. Helena Highway S.
963-3542

Hanns Kornell Cellars
Larkmead Lane
WOodward 3-2334

Charles Krug Winery
    (C. Mondavi and Sons)
P. O. Box 191
WOodward 3-2761

Louis M. Martini
P. O. Box 112
WOodward 3-2736

Mont La Salle Vineyards
226-5566

Nichelini Vineyard
State Highway 128
963-3357

Souverain Cellars
P. O. Box 348
WOodward 3-3688

Sutter Home Winery
State Highway 29
WOodward 3-3104

Sacramento County

ELK GROVE
Gibson Wine Company
P. O. Drawer E
MUrray 5-9594

FLORIN
James Frasinetti & Sons
First Street
GArden 8-2421

SACRAMENTO
Mills Winery
9910 Folsom Boulevard
363-9959

San Bernadino County

ALTA LOMA
Opici Winery Inc.
P. O. Box 56
YUkon 7-2710

CUCAMONGA
Aggazzotti Winery
11929 Foothill Boulevard
YUkon 7-1657

Cucamonga Winery
Rochester Avenue
YUkon 7-2509

Cucamonga Vineyard Company
10013 Eighth Street
YUkon 7-1716

San Bernadino County (contd.)

CUCAMONGA (contd.)
    Thomas Vineyards
    8916 Foothill Boulevard
    YUkon 7-1612

ETIWANDA
    Cucamonga Top Winery
    12737 Foothill Boulevard
    987-2786

FONTANA
    Louis Cherpin
    15567 Valley Boulevard (U.S. 99)
    VAlley 2-4103

GUASTI
    Brookside Vineyard Company
        (Assumption Abbey Winery)
    9900 A Street
    YUkon 3-2787

San Diego County

ESCONDIDO
    Ferrara Winery
    1120 West 15th Street
    SHerwood 5-7632

San Joaquin County

ACAMPO
    Barengo Cellars
    East End Orange Street
    ENdicott 9-2746

    California Wine Association
    ENdicott 9-3653

San Joaquin County (contd.)

ESCALON
    Cadlolo Winery
    1124 California Street
    838-2457

LOCKEFORD
    Lockeford Winery
    Locke Road
    RAymond 7-5562

LODI
    Alex's Winery
    R.F.D. 2, Box 227
    ENdicott 8-3160

    East-Side Winery
    1600 Victor Road
    ENdicott 9-4768

    Guild Wine Company
    1 Winemaster's Way
    ENdicott 8-5151

    Lodi Winery, Inc.
    P. O. Box 188
    ENdicott 8-0179

    Woodbridge Vineyard Association
    J 4614 W. Turner Road
    ENdicott 9-2614

MANTECA
    Sam-Jasper Winery
    U.S. Route 99
    TAlbot 3-5616

San Joaquin County (contd.)

RIPON
> Franzia Brothers Winery
> Yosemite Avenue
> 599-4251

San Luis Obispo County

TEMPLETON
> Pesenti Winery
> Vineyard Drive
> 434-1030
>
> Rotta Winery
> Winery Road
> 434-1389
>
> York Mountain Winery
> York Mountain Road
> 238-3491

Santa Clara County

CUPERTINO
> Ridge Vineyards*
> 17100 Monte Bello Rd.
> 867-3233

GILROY
> Bertero Winery
> Route 1, Box 53
> VInewood 2-3032
>
> Bonesio Winery
> 842-2601
>
> Los Altos Vineyards
> Box 247
> 842-5649

* By appointment only.

Santa Clara County (contd.)

LOS GATOS
> Almadén Vineyards
> Blossom Hill Road
> ANdrews 9-1312
>
> David Bruce*
> 21439 Bear Creek Road
> 354-4214
>
> Novitiate of Los Gatos
> College Avenue
> 354-3737

MORGAN HILL
> E. Guglielmo Winery
> East Main Avenue
> 779-3064
>
> Pedrizetti Winery
> San Padro Avenue
> 779-3710
>
> Richert & Sons, Inc.
> 1120 N. El Camino Real
> 779-3919

MOUNTAIN VIEW
> Gemello Winery
> 2003 El Camino Real
> WHitecliff 8-7723

SAN JOSE
> Mirassou Vineyards
> Route 3, Box 344
> 251-5030

* By appointment only.

Santa Clara County (contd.)

SAN MARTIN
San Martin Vineyards Company
P. O. Box 53
MUtual 3-2672

SARATOGA
Martin Ray, Inc.*
UNion 7-3205

Paul Masson Vineyards
13150 Saratoga Avenue
ALpine 2-0400

Santa Cruz County

SOQUEL
Nicasio Vineyards*
Nicasio Way
GArden 3-1073

Bargetto's Santa Cruz Winery
3535 N. Main Street
475-2258

WATSONVILLE
S. Martinelli & Company
P. O. Box 549, 227 Third Street
724-1126

Solano County

FAIRFIELD
Cadenasso Winery
Box 22
HArrison 5-5845

* By appointment only.

Solano County (contd.)

SUISUN CITY
Wooden Valley Winery
Route 1, Box 124
HArrison 5-3962

Sonoma County

ASTI
Italian Swiss Colony
P. O. Box 1
TWinbrook 4-2541

CLOVERDALE
Bandiera Wines
155 Cherry Creek Road
TWinbrook 4-5887

FORESTVILLE
Russian River Vineyards
5700 Gravenstein Highway N.
887-2243

GEYSERVILLE
J. Pedroncelli Winery
1220 Canyon Road
857-3619

GUERNEVILLE
Korbel Winery
Korbel Station
887-2294

HEALDSBURG
Cambiaso Winery
1141 Grant Avenue
IDlewood 3-1513

Sonoma County (contd.)

HEALDSBURG (contd.)
L. Foppiano Wine Company
P. O. Box 606
433-1937

SANTA ROSA
Martini & Prati Wines, Inc.
2191 Laguna Road
VAlley 3-2404

SONOMA
Buena Vista Vineyards
Old Winery Road
WEbster 8-8504

Samuele Sebastiani
388 Fourth Street
WEbster 8-5532

WINDSOR
Windsor Vineyards
(Tiburon Vintners)
P. O. Box 57
433-5545

Stanislaus County

SALIDA
Pirrone Wine Cellars
U.S. Route 99
545-0704

Tulare County

CUTLER
California Growers Wineries
P. O. Box 38
LAwrence 8-3055

Tuolumne County

COLUMBIA
Columbia Cellars
Parrots Ferry Road
532-9214

SONORA
Butler Winery
Rt. 3, Box 357
586-4384

Index

INDEX

Brand names are printed in *italics*. **Bold** type indicates
pages where main discussion of winery or wine appears.

12/80 under $4.00

Stoney Creek chablis
Los Hermanos Chenin blanc + cabernet
San Martin - Rhine
  "   "   Calif. burgundy

Vouvray
Entre-deux-mer
Bon de Venice ?